THE SEVEN CHECKPOINTS

for Student Leaders

Seven Principles Every Teenager Needs to Know

THE SEVEN CHECKPOINTS

for Student Leaders

ANDY STANLEY
STUART HALL

HOWARD BOOKS
A DIVISION OF SIMON & SCHUSTER, INC.
New York · Nashville · London · Toronto · Sydney

Howard Books
A Division of Simon & Schuster, Inc.
1230 Avenue of the Americas
New York, NY 10020

First Howard Books trade paperback edition April 2011

HOWARD and colophon are trademarks of Simon & Schuster, Inc.

For information about special discounts for bulk purchases,
please contact Simon & Schuster Special Sales at 1-866-506-1949
or business@simonandschuster.com.

The Simon & Schuster Speakers Bureau can bring authors to your live event.
For more information or to book an event, contact the Simon & Schuster Speakers Bureau
at 1-866-248-3049 or visit our website at www.simonspeakers.com.

Designed by Ruth Lee-Mui

Manufactured in the United States of America

10   9   8   7   6   5   4   3   2   1

Library of Congress Cataloging-in-Publication Data

Stanley, Andy.
    The seven checkpoints for student leaders : seven principles every teenager needs to know /
Andy Stanley, Stuart Hall.
        p. cm.
    1. Christian education of teenagers.   I. Hall, Stuart, 1968—   II. Title.
    BV1485.S69 2011
    259'.23—dc22
2010042108

ISBN 978-1-4391-8933-7
ISBN 978-1-4516-2845-6 (ebook)

This is a revised edition of a work previously published as The Seven Checkpoints for Youth Leaders.

To the student ministry teams at
North Point Community Church,
Buckhead Church, and
Browns Bridge Community Church

Contents

Contents

Foreword

I began to write this foreword with the idea that student ministry is a rapidly changing, hard-to-grasp "thing," evolving so fast that it's almost impossible to stay on the cutting edge. But is that really true?

Andy Stanley and I met the summer before seventh grade. During the height of a shaving-cream free-for-all, I, being the smallest kid in camp, took cover under a bunk bed, fearing for my life. Funny thing. Andy was already under there, his eyes as big as mine. We connected. In the heat of battle, our keen survival skills initiated a bond that has remained to this day.

Back then student ministry was interesting. We had never heard the word *worship*; we just sang songs. The only missionary we knew of was named Lottie Moon. Lottie Moon? To have a spiritual high, you had to have a really big fire and throw something into it. Sure, we "counted the cost," but the idea of dying for our faith was a concept that never crossed our minds. Our biggest concern was that the Cokes and Krispy Kremes be there on Sunday morning. Life was good.

So maybe a little has changed. But a lot hasn't. We had a student minister (they called her the youth director back then) who loved us, teachers who fed us, role models who inspired us, a pastor who poured God's Word into us, and environments that shaped us.

These days people claim the stakes are higher, but how could they be higher than they were? Every day is critical to God. The wisdom writer said, "There's nothing new under the sun." I've lived long enough to agree.

The keys to effective student ministry are the same today as they were back then. First, we need innovative leaders, those who blaze a trail with fresh creativity and not just a rehashed imitation of the current culture. Second, we must have a belief in our students' capacity to grasp more, a conviction that they can access and experience the deeper things of God. Third, we as leaders must have a genuine and living faith, empowering us to "show the way" and not just "tell the way." And fourth, we must have a clear strategy so that at the end of the day we don't just have a pile of expended energy but rather the assurance that we've accomplished the goal.

That's why what Andy Stanley and Stuart Hall have done in these pages is vital. Effective strategy helps us worry less about what's changing around us and focus more on what will always be true. Andy is the most strategic person I know. He's amazing to watch. He lives out what he has written down. So let him lead you and help you channel your passion and sacrifice into a pathway to progress.

One last thing (and this is for us all): let's *live* these principles first and *teach* them second. That way we'll know at least one person in the group is getting it!

That's a built-in guarantee of success.

Louie Giglio

Preface

After thirty years of working with teenagers, I am convinced that there are seven basic principles every student should understand, commit to memory, and embrace before graduating and leaving the safety of home and student ministry.

These seven student-specific principles are the irreducible minimum. They are the must-know, can't-do-without principles. They are not all that is important. But they are what is most important for students.

When I was a student pastor, I invested a great deal of time looking for useful curricula. I spent countless hours piecing together interesting talks. I tried hard to find good camp speakers. I threw a lot of helpful information at my students in those days. I'm sure some of it stuck. But how much? Which parts?

Were the *things* that stuck with them the things that *needed* to stick?

Taking Stock

After I graduated my fourth senior class, I decided it was time for some pointed evaluation. That's when I discovered I had no tool with which to evaluate my ministry. We were growing numerically. That kept all the higher-ups happy. But I had no way of knowing how effectively I was instilling life-changing truth into the hearts of my students.

That fourth graduating class sat under my teaching from ninth through twelfth grade. But what did they learn? Did I communicate, or did I simply cover a lot of material?

At that point I gathered my staff (both of them) and began asking questions:

- ✓ If we could permanently imprint anything we wanted upon our students' minds, what would it be?

- ✓ What do they need to know? What is the irreducible minimum?

- ✓ When everybody else is "doing it," what's going to keep him from joining in?

- ✓ When she is sitting in a dorm room during her freshman year, contemplating her options for the

evening, what principles or truths should drift
through her mind in that potentially defining
moment?

This ongoing dialogue lasted for several months. I would throw out one or two of these questions for discussion at every leadership meeting. Whenever I met with other student pastors, I asked them what they believed were the most important concepts for students to embrace. Eventually I compiled a list of twelve principles. After presenting these twelve truths to several trusted men and women in student ministry, I reduced the list to nine and eventually to seven.

Selective Memory

Let's face it. Our students will forget most of what we teach them. But, hopefully, they will remember *something*. We have wasted a whole lot of time preparing and teaching if they don't! And assuming they will remember something, doesn't it make sense that we determine what they will remember?

After all, God has positioned us in the lives of our students as leaders, mentors, and friends. For a few short but strategic years, we have the opportunity and responsibility to shape their thinking. And in doing so, we have the privilege of helping set their life trajectories.

The Student Ministry Dilemma

No doubt you have gained some proficiency in creating exciting and attractive environments for students. But as you know, both *context* and *content* are crucial for effective student ministry. The context—the environment—is what keeps them coming back. The content—what we communicate—is what equips them for life. If you are like me, the content side of the equation is what drew you into student ministry. You wanted to see kids' lives changed. But you quickly learned that without the right context, there wouldn't be any lives to change!

Consequently, you have been forced to spend a great deal of time and energy (and money!) creating attractive environments for students. To compound the challenge, the success of your ministry is probably judged on your ability to attract students. You don't get to hire extra staff based on the spiritual development of your students; you get staff support when the numbers demand it.

Bottom line: the context of your ministry has tended to demand most of your attention. So, like me, you have probably come to the end of a stretch of ministry and wondered, *What did they learn?* You know what they *heard*. But what did they take away? Sure, they will remember the events and the people who were "there for them." But did they walk away with the tools and the truths they will need to survive and thrive in the world beyond high school?

The tyranny of the urgent and the quest for a larger budget are facts of student ministry life. You and I have to keep creating those high-energy, pack-'em-in environments. If we have a room that will seat one hundred students, we need to do everything we can to fill it up.

Once the room is full, however, let's make sure the content we throw at them sticks. Let's make it memorable. Let's make it transformational. And let's keep coming back to a handful of concepts over and over until our students dream them in their sleep. That's where the seven checkpoints come in.

Recycled Truth

This book is designed to provide you with the content for those environments you spend so much time and energy creating. My goal in writing *The Seven Checkpoints* is to give you seven principles around which you can organize the content of your entire student ministry.

I have developed two models to choose from—a three-year model and a four-year model. The idea is that in three or four years you can cycle several times through all seven principles. Each of these plans will incorporate your Sunday small-group times, weekend retreats, and summer camps. The seven principles have been reduced to seven memorable phrases—phrases that you can use to pepper your leadership training, counseling, teaching, and speaking.

Imagine meeting with the parents of your students and showing them the seven principles that serve as the foundation for all you will teach their kids.

Imagine having a content calendar that you can use to guide the development of your activity calendar throughout the year.

Imagine having a handful of carefully crafted principles to choose from in developing the theme of every camp or retreat.

These are just a few of the advantages of adopting the seven-checkpoints strategy. But the greatest advantage is this: You will know that you are maximizing your input into the lives of the students God has entrusted to your care. You will know that you are changing lives. And isn't that why you got into student ministry in the first place?

The Seven Irreducible Minimums of Student Ministry

SEVEN PRINCIPLES EVERY TEENAGER NEEDS TO KNOW

We must learn to use what is cultural
to communicate what is timeless.

Seven Irreducible Minimums
of Student Ministry

It is a great time in history to work with teenagers.

Student ministry has evolved into a profession of professionals. The fight for today's student culture is so intense that the position of student minister, once considered the lowest rung on the job ladder, now commands special recognition.

We have entered the race with the likes of MTV and Hollywood for the minds and hearts of teenagers. In doing so, our need for context and student-friendly environments dominates our thoughts, training events, and philosophies of ministry. We put on camps and conferences and create weekly environments that rival rock concerts in sight and sound.

In order to communicate with teenagers in their language, Christian music is no longer on the periphery but in the music mainstream. Quality television shows help students understand who Jesus is and how to deal with the issues that are unique to their stage of life.

The Heart of the Matter

These new approaches are refreshing. They are especially refreshing to those of us who spent countless hours trying to convince the generation ahead of us that an anapestic beat wouldn't send kids to hell.

But the pendulum has swung past the point of balance. While the *context* has consumed us, the *content* has taken a backseat. We spend little time determining what our students need to know before they graduate from our ministry. We spend our days designing camp shirts and planning activities, and what we want our students to know often gets lost in the shuffle.

Think for a moment about the students who just graduated from your ministry. In the spaces below, list the four or five key principles you believe they walked away with because of the time they spent under your leadership. _____

_____

_____

_____

_____

_____

Are these the things you intentionally taught them, or did they pick them up accidentally?

The Ever-Raging Battle

Our students live in an entertainment-oriented culture. Just about every morsel of relevant or irrelevant information they pick up is designed to stimulate their senses. If it's not entertaining, they aren't interested.

This is why we have rushed to create high-energy, entertainment-driven contexts for our ministries. And we should, as long as the content doesn't suffer. But it is hard to stay content focused when the "show" takes so much time and energy.

So how do we keep substance in the driver's seat? What can we do to ensure that the music doesn't drown out the message? How do we ensure that our students walk away from our student ministries equipped to enter the next chapters of their lives?

Context versus Content

Again, this book is not about context. It is about substance. It is about content. It's about *what* you should communicate to your students, not *how* to communicate it. This book is about instilling timeless principles into the hearts of teenagers to better equip them to live in their ever-changing culture.

A huge frustration that most student leaders face is a lack of great curricula for discipleship. If you are like me, hundreds of marketing pieces advertising new teaching materials come across your desk every year. There is no shortage of resources. However, there is a lack of a systematic plan around which to implement our curriculum choices.

Timeless Methods

We tend to plan our environments and events first and then decide the content to be taught. By adapting your ministry to the seven checkpoints presented in this book, the content will dictate how you plan and create environments. We speak freely in the church today about the need to preserve the message while adjusting our methods to reach a generation of students. But in our attempts to remain methodologically relevant, we have not been intentional about the messages.

Think about the time and energy you spend planning the *context* for your summer camp or student retreat versus the time and energy you put into the *content*. Isn't it true that you spend the majority of your time creating the right environment and then leave the development of content to a guest speaker—someone who doesn't even know your kids?

Your small-group environment is predictable as well: chairs in rows (sometimes circles) for students and a lectern for the teacher. Perhaps you have doughnuts and juice on one table and quiet-time guides, event brochures, and announcement sheets on another. Your adult student leaders stand along the back wall or sit in the last row of chairs. You trust a publisher to provide a lesson for you to teach, and you have no idea what that will be from one quarter to the next. In many cases, the publisher chooses what your students should learn, not you!

Of course, we leave room for the Holy Spirit to move, and we trust the speaker and the writers, but perhaps the reason there is so much "room" and so much "trust" is that *we're* not sure what we want our students to remember, understand, and apply.

What have become foundational for us are our *methods*, not our content. We have gradually put the proverbial "cart before the horse," and the results sit in big church every Sunday morning in the shape of young adults who have a what's-in-it-for-me attitude and a weak biblical foundation.

Try It

We invested many hours developing a strategy that would be content driven. What has evolved is a ministry model that creates environments based on seven key biblical principles, or "checkpoints," as we refer to them.

Again, *content* drives our *context*. We are still committed to creating relevant environments. But the environments must support the content. We have discovered that once we have identified *what* we want students to walk away with, creating more focused and effective environments is much easier.

After all, it is one thing to put together a summer camp. It is another thing to create the optimal five-day environment for teenagers to rethink their whole approach to friendship. It is one thing to organize a winter retreat. But the stakes get higher when the goal is to create the optimal setting for students to examine their attitudes toward the authorities God has put in their lives. It is one thing to plan a month's worth of Sunday-school or small-group content. But what if the goal that month is to motivate your students to adopt an others-first approach to relationships?

When content is the focus, the context is still vitally important. This approach will motivate you and your leadership to raise the bar programmatically. Camp is camp. Sunday school is Sunday school. But what if your leaders viewed these regularly scheduled events as the context for imparting seven life-changing principles? Suddenly the stakes are higher. Now camp, Sunday school, and the winter retreat are necessary means to a predetermined end.

Good Intentions

The Seven Checkpoints is an intentional, systematic approach to discipleship focused on the *content* of discipleship. As stated earlier, these seven, student-specific principles are the irreducible minimum.

As you begin to journey through the pages of this book, you will find that each checkpoint asks a *critical question*. Each question forces you, the leader, to evaluate your students based on that question. Each question also presents a *key passage* from the Bible that serves as the timeless foundation for the question. Each checkpoint is stated as an easy-to-remember principle. This helps you and your students remember the checkpoint in a simple, yet powerful, statement of truth.

Here's a quick overview of *The Seven Checkpoints*:

Checkpoint #1: Authentic Faith

This focuses on a correct understanding of faith. Faith is confidence that God is who he says he is and that he will do all he has promised to do.

Principle: *God can be trusted; he will do all he has promised to do.*
Critical Question: *Are your students trusting God with the critical areas of their lives?*
Key Passage: *Proverbs 3:5–6*

Checkpoint #2: Spiritual Disciplines

A student's devotional life is the focus of this checkpoint. The apostle Paul assures us that transformation begins with a renewed mind. As students begin to renew their minds to the truths of Scripture, their attitudes and behaviors will change.

Principle: *If I can see as God sees, I will do as God says.*
Critical Question: *Are your students developing consistent devotional and prayer lives?*
Key Passage: *Romans 12:2*

Checkpoint #3: Moral Boundaries

Purity paves the way to intimacy. One of the most important things a student can do is establish limits. Students need to learn how to protect their bodies and emotions by honoring God's plan for sex and morality.

Principle: *Purity paves the way for intimacy.*

Critical Question: *Are your students establishing and maintaining moral boundaries?*

Key Passage: *1 Thessalonians 4:3–8*

Checkpoint #4: Meaningful Friendships

The people our students associate with the most will determine the direction and quality of their lives. This principle focuses on helping our teenagers build healthy friendships and avoid unhealthy ones.

Principle: *Our friends determine the direction and quality of our lives.*

Critical Question: *Are your students establishing healthy friendships and avoiding unhealthy ones?*

Key Passage: *Proverbs 13:20*

Checkpoint #5: Wise Choices

In light of their past experiences, current circumstances, and future hopes and dreams, students need to ask themselves, "What is the wise thing to do?" Good decision making is more than simply choosing between right and wrong. This principle focuses on the need for wisdom in decision making.

Principle: *Walk wisely in a fool's world.*

Critical Question: *Are your students making wise decisions?*

Key Passage: *Ephesians 5:15–17*

Checkpoint #6: Ultimate Authority

Freedom and authority are often viewed as opposing concepts. But the Scriptures teach that freedom is found under authority. This principle focuses on the need for students to stay under the authorities that God has placed over them.

Principle: *Maximum freedom is found under God's authority.*

Critical Question: *Are your students submitting to the authorities God has placed over them?*

Key Passage: *Romans 13:1–2*

Checkpoint #7: Others First

Selfishness comes naturally. Selflessness must be learned. The hallmark of believers is their willingness to put the needs of others ahead of their own. This principle addresses our students' propensity toward selfishness and self-centeredness.

Principle: *Consider others before yourself.*

Critical Question: *Do your students consider others before themselves?*

Key Passage: *Philippians 2:3–11*

You may be thinking, *I'm not so sure about this.* And you may be wondering, *Are you suggesting that we teach these same seven concepts over and over?* The answer is yes. We are suggesting that you develop all of your teaching environments around *The Seven Checkpoints.* I know it doesn't sound feasible, but it is.

Most student pastors have no plan as to what they are going to teach and when they are going to teach it. The "buffet" approach to curriculum is the popular plan of the day—decide what is most relevant, most current, or most fresh on the mind of the student pastor and then teach it. Even if you do not adopt the strategy proposed in this book, you have to adopt *a plan*. Simply reacting to the latest book you read or sermon you hear does not constitute a plan for packing the bags of the students God has entrusted to you. You need to get your primary volunteers or staff in a room and ask the question, "What are the principles that we want to teach over the next few years?" And you need to make a conscious decision, followed up by a strategic plan, to make sure that you teach those principles repeatedly. This plan will be the guardrails that keep your ministry on track.

Repetition

When we have presented this strategy in seminars, leaders often voice a concern about the wisdom of repeating the same things over and over. The concern is that repeating the same principles year after year spells doom for a student's interest in the things of God. That concern is valid. The problem, however, is that it assumes that repetition is the reason students get bored. In most cases, the problem is not the repetition; it is the *presentation*.

It has been my experience that a lifeless presentation and the tendency to try to cover too much information in a short amount of time cause boredom. Repetition has little to do with it. Repetition is how we learn. When my son was five years old, he learned how to kneeboard behind a jet ski. He didn't accomplish that feat on the first try. It was only after an hour of repeating instructions like "lean back, extend your arms, and shift your weight" (try explaining that to a five-year-old) that he was enjoying skimming on top of the water with a huge smile on his face. Repetition brought success.

I have never met a student who, after hearing one talk on trusting God, fully understood the depths of that issue and obeyed God in that area for the rest of his life. Repetition has transformed many areas of our lives spiritually, emotionally, and physically. Don't fear repetition.

Curriculum

One of the other concerns that is voiced from time to time is, "Where are we going to find enough material on these seven topics to fill out a four- or six-year curriculum menu?" Actually, we wondered the same thing.

What we discovered is that once we established a grid for the content of our student ministry, we knew exactly what curriculum to look for. Once we narrowed our focus, we were surprised at how much material had been written on these seven common themes.

In addition to published material, we have had success

developing some of our own curriculum. Again, once we established the basic subject matter, it wasn't difficult to recruit several of our seasoned teachers to begin developing lesson plans. You may be surprised how eager your leadership will be to help fill the gaps in your curriculum menu once you give them some basic parameters.

Using the Checkpoints

We cycle the seven checkpoints through our middle school and high school ministries annually. As we plan our year, we look at the following environments and ask the question, "Which of the checkpoints would be best communicated in each of these settings?"

Small Groups

Chances are you have some type of small-group environment for your students. Our small-group ministry for high school students, *InsideOut*, meets on Sunday afternoons. *Transit*, our small-group environment for middle school, meets on Sunday mornings. In each of these environments, we use a master teacher for the first twenty minutes of teaching time. The speaker focuses on the checkpoint that is being discussed for the month.* Students will then go to their small groups to discuss

*The number of weeks allotted to each checkpoint varies based upon grade level and the topic itself. See Appendix 1 for an overview of our teaching schedule.

it in detail. Small group leaders focus on facilitating discussion rather than teaching the checkpoint.

The goal of *InsideOut* and *Transit* is for students to walk away with one idea and one point of application. By focusing on one principle, students are more apt to grasp and *apply* truth instead of merely *hearing* truth.

Camps and Retreats

As we look at our ministry year, we use the seven checkpoints to determine the themes of our camps and retreats. By building your camp or retreat around one checkpoint, your students will have at least one entire weekend or week per year totally devoted to a checkpoint. For example, *Vertical Reality,* our fall retreat, always focuses on Checkpoint #1, Authentic Faith. We have found that a weekend-retreat setting is optimal for reinforcing the spiritual disciplines.

There are several advantages to choosing a single checkpoint for a camp or weekend retreat. Once you have identified the focus of your content, you can be strategic in your selection of a camp speaker. Second, it gives everybody on your planning team direction for worship, breakout groups, and devotional material. Last, you are able to clearly and succinctly communicate to parents the message of the week or weekend. How motivated would parents be to make sure their kids were signed up for camp if you announced that the theme was going to be "Developing and Maintaining Healthy Friendships"? Imagine their excitement when you explain that the principle you hope to instill in the hearts of their kids is that their friends have the potential to determine the direction and quality of their lives.

Service Projects

A third environment that is conducive to reinforcing the seven checkpoints is a service project (e.g., mission trips, backyard Bible clubs). We use this type of environment to focus our students' attention on Checkpoint #7, Others First.

Our primary others-first environment is *Student Impact*. It is an experiential learning environment that gives students opportunities to discover and then use their gifts to serve in our church on Sunday mornings.

By serving as small-group leaders for preschoolers, children, or middle schoolers, students put others first every Sunday morning. Our high-school students also serve on our various worship and production teams. As part of *Student Impact,* they are required to participate in ongoing training that is designed to help them understand their responsibility to put others first through the use of their gifts and the investment of their time.

Total Integration

As student ministers, Stuart and I focused our teaching on the irreducible minimums represented in *The Seven Checkpoints.*

We discovered the value of focusing and refocusing the minds and hearts of our students on a handful of principles that would prepare them for the next chapter in their lives. Unfortunately, we weren't able to integrate these seven essentials into the overall frameworks of our student ministries.

At our North Point Ministries campuses, we have taken *The Seven Checkpoints* to the next level. Thanks to the vision and leadership of our student ministry staff, these seven principles have become the core for all of our student-oriented environments. Content is driving our context. And nobody is complaining about the repetition.

Looking Back

When you signed on for student ministry, producing events and shuffling papers was probably the last thing on your mind. You wanted then, as you do now, to make a difference in the lives of teenagers. But it wasn't long before you found yourself drowning in a sea of paperwork and administrative duties. If you are wired anything like I am, by the time you get camp organized, you are not even sure you want to go!

And while you sort through the "important" stuff that has to be done, students are coming and going. Growing up. Breaking up. Graduating. Moving on. Chances are, as busy as you might have been during their tenure in your student ministry, they will never forget you. But surely you want them to remember more than just you! You didn't respond to God's call to student ministry so you would be remembered. You signed on to shape the attitudes and beliefs of a generation of kids. You responded to this call for the sake of the one kid you might help to avoid the pitfalls of young adult life.

I believe the principles embodied in *The Seven Checkpoints* are essential to the relational, emotional, and spiritual health of our teenagers. You touch on most of these topics from time to time anyway. Why not embrace a plan that will help you and your leadership integrate these seven core ideas into everything you are doing in your ministry?

When we were writing this book, Stuart told me a story that I think illustrates the impact we all want to make on at least a handful of students that God entrusts to our care. More important, it illustrates what can happen when a student minister refuses to settle for simply being remembered.

Kellee and I had been married exactly one year when we agreed to move from Mobile, Alabama, to Bossier City, Louisiana. I had taken a position as minister to students at First Baptist Church of Bossier City. We were there for five wonderful years.

About four months after starting in Bossier, we met Kevin. Kevin came to church every Sunday on the church bus. It never failed that I would have the daunting task of rounding up Kevin and his friends as they tried to skip church and start trouble. Our confrontation came one Sunday in Cross Training, our student Bible study on Sunday mornings. Kevin and his cohorts were sitting directly behind Kellee and making too much noise. When Kellee turned and nicely asked Kevin to quiet down, he introduced her to an array of filthy curse words that make Chris Rock sound like Mother Teresa.

Unfortunately, it cost Kevin his weekly trip to our church for a month. Those bus drivers didn't play!

Kevin's parents were not wealthy. He had a younger brother who was autistic. Kevin has since admitted to me that he struggled with not being proud of his family or poor upbringing. He has never owned fashionable clothes. People have always made fun of him. In the world's view, Kevin was born without much of a chance to succeed in life.

Slowly but surely, Kevin began to change. Some of our students befriended him, and he became an active part of the student ministry. God began to transform his life, and I had the privilege of watching.

Kevin made the varsity football team at Airline High School, and it was always a blast to watch him pace the sidelines on Friday nights. He was the consummate team player, and his teammates could count on his encouragement and support. Although he rarely stepped foot on the field, he had the heart of a champion.

I had the privilege, along with his small-group leader and friends, of investing in Kevin for four years. He spent many weekends at my house during his senior year. He was honest about his struggles. He was burdened for his friends. He made me laugh about why the girl of his dreams would never give in to his romantic attempts at winning her heart. He was so hungry to know God in a much deeper way. He battled with tough choices.

I must admit there were times when his knock at my door made my head drop, but I never regretted the time I spent with him. I would always walk away from those times so grateful for the fact that God had allowed Kevin to enter my life. Little did I know that helping him understand authentic faith, practice spiritual disciplines, establish moral boundaries and meaningful friendships, make wise choices, submit to God-given authority, and think of others before himself would make such a lasting impression on his life.

After graduation, Kevin decided to attend Louisiana State University in Baton Rouge. During his four years at LSU, he mentored junior-high students at the church he attended, played rugby for LSU, and was a volunteer football coach for University High School. When he informed me that he planned to major in pre-law, I must admit I laughed deep down.

I'm not laughing anymore.

Kevin graduated with a perfect 4.0 average.

He was accepted to Harvard University's law school.

He wanted to become a lawyer and give most of what he earned to furthering the gospel of Christ.

Stuart concluded his story with this remark: Kevin is one of the reasons I believe in these seven principles.

I couldn't agree more.

Checking In

Seven Principles Every Teenager Needs
to Know

Bible Study Assignment

1. Read 1 and 2 Timothy, and highlight those places where Paul invested these seven principles in Timothy's life. Mark each place with the appropriate checkpoint.

Questions

✓ If parents walked into your office today and asked what you are investing in their student, could you give them a clear and definite answer? What would you say?_____

_____

_____

_____

✓ Why do you think Paul was repetitious with Timothy in his discipleship of him? _____

_____

_____

_____

✓ Do you consider your ministry effective? Why or why not?_

_____

_____

_____

✓ Think back to the last four summer camps or retreats you have done. What were the themes and principles taught at those camps? _____

_____

_____

✓ If you were to adopt the seven principles in this book, what would be the greatest obstacle you would face in implementing them? _____

_____

_____

✓ Take out your calendar and daily schedule. What consumes most of your time? Are those things about effectiveness? _____

_____

_____

✓ Journal your thoughts, questions, and comments from what you've read in this overview of the checkpoints._____

_____

_____

_____

Checkpoint #1

Authentic Faith

GOD CAN BE TRUSTED

I'm the first one to admit that I am somewhat cynical

when it comes to faith.

I envy people who can just let go and totally commit.

I, on the other hand, can't even hear the title of the show

Touched by an Angel

without thinking that a professional baseball player

is being sued for sexual harassment.

—Dennis Miller, *I Rant, Therefore I Am*

Checkpoint

Authentic Faith

Critical Questions

Are your students trusting God with

the critical areas of their lives?

Principle

God can be trusted; he will do all he has promised to do.

Key Passage

Proverbs 3:5–6

Authentic Faith
DILEMMA

As Christians, we are instructed to live by *faith*. But what does that mean? What is *faith*? If we have a whole lot of *faith*, does that mean God will answer all our prayers? And why does our *faith* go down the tubes when things go badly?

Since faith is foundational in the process of spiritual formation, it is imperative that our students understand what faith is and what it isn't. Confusion over the definition of faith is rampant in the Christian community. Faith is spoken of as if it is some kind of force or power. Confusion in this one area is the primary reason so many students abandon Christianity. It is the reason students have such difficulty trusting God with every area of their lives. It is also the reason so many of our students are unsure of their salvation. They raise their hands at camp to indicate they are receiving Christ as their Savior. At the end of this checkpoint, we will address the subject of saving faith. Before we do, however, let's talk about faith in general.

Shattered Faith

Like me, you know students who would readily admit that they *used to be* Christians. They *used to go* to church, but not anymore.

They *used to* believe, but not anymore. Many of our students have parents who would acknowledge that they used to be Christians but something happened. Now they don't believe. They "lost" their faith.

There are two things that shatter a student's faith. The first is poor choices. When believing students veer off course morally, relationally, or ethically, they are immediately confronted with waves of guilt. There are only two ways to get rid of guilt: ask for forgiveness and change your behavior; or change your belief system. If we can convince ourselves that there is nothing wrong with what we are doing, our guilt is greatly diminished. Changing how we believe is always easier than changing how we behave.

Many of the "used to believe" students running around in our student ministries traded in their faith for more convenient lifestyles. When students change what they believe in order to justify their behavior, it says something about the nature of their faith. Obviously, they had shallow faith. It was rooted in convenience rather than conviction. It was based on what worked for them at the time. This kind of faith can be summarized this way: What's happening *now*, what I'm feeling *now*, determines what I believe for *now*.

The second reason students abandon Christianity is unexplainable tragedy. By that, I mean a tragedy that does not fit the character of God or the Christian faith, as one believes it to be. It is difficult to believe in a good God when bad things happen.

When students are confronted with tragedy, they ask, "How could a good God allow this to happen? Why didn't he stop it?"

The inability to figure this out is why many students abandon Christianity. When this happens, it is evident that their faith is rooted in the present as well. Again, they are living by . . .

> # What's happening now, what I'm feeling now, determines what I believe for now.

As long as their faith is grounded in what they see around them and what they experience, their faith will be fragile. It is nothing more than circumstantial faith.

Circumstantial Faith

Circumstantial faith is fragile. Circumstantial faith is supported by our ability (or inability) to interpret events. Lauren prays and prays and prays to God for help in passing a test—and she fails. So Lauren interprets that to mean that God doesn't answer prayer or that he is mad at her or that he just can't be trusted. Her faith is impacted by her interpretation of the circumstances around her.

Like the rest of us, students are prone to misinterpret events. God's faithfulness and character are never predicated upon the unfolding of circumstances. Yet, for many in the Christian community, the ever-changing landscape of circumstances defines God. Ask a four-year-old on the way to the doctor for a tetanus shot if his daddy loves him. He would have his doubts. But years later, ask that same child about the doctor visit. He will have a completely different perspective. Just as a child cannot correctly judge his parent's character based on a trip to the doctor, we dare not draw conclusions about God's goodness based on the immediate circumstances of our lives.

Another reason circumstantial faith is so fragile is that our frames of reference are too small. It is hard for us to look at the significance of events in the context of a lifetime, much less put those events in the context of eternity. Students are stressed over things like taking a test, getting a date, winning a game, or being left out. Neutrogena and Oxy 10 are making a killing off students' stress!

The Old Testament's Joseph spent fifteen years as a slave in Egypt after being sold by his brothers. Yet, it was all a part of the beautiful tapestry that God was weaving behind the scenes. Moses spent forty years in the wilderness before God sent him back to Egypt and introduced some purpose into what was a seemingly purposeless existence.

Yet, if God doesn't answer our students' prayers by next week, they wonder if he even exists. If they don't see God at work in their immediate circumstances, they lose their confidence in him. All of this stems from a faulty understanding of faith.

So, what are students to build their faith on? If not their immediate circumstances, then what?

The Foundation of our Faith

The foundation of our faith is a person, not a recent event. The foundation of our faith is Jesus Christ. As leaders, we must redirect the faith of our students away from current events and fasten it to the One in whom they can securely place their trust.

In the book of Hebrews, the author addresses a group of Jewish Christians who were being pressured by the Jewish community—and circumstances in general—to abandon their faith. They had been ostracized from the synagogue, which was the hub of their society. In their world, there were no practical benefits to being Christian. It was costing them socially and financially.

And to make things worse, they had been led to believe that Jesus was coming back soon. And so far it had been a big no-show! Consequently, they were beginning to doubt whether or not this Christianity thing was for real.

So the author writes this letter to encourage his readers not to abandon their faith. The basis of his argument is the identity of Christ. For three chapters he presents a mountain of evidence pointing toward the conclusion that Christ is God. The writer declares that we believe because Jesus walked on this earth, claimed to be God, gave us evidence supporting his claim, died for our sin, rose from the dead, and went back to heaven in front of hundreds of witnesses. And he concludes his summary by stating, *"Therefore, since we have a great high priest who has gone through the heavens, Jesus the Son of God, let us hold firmly to the faith we profess"* (Hebrews 4:14).

If Christ is who he says he is, then we don't need to worry when bad things happen. If Jesus really died for the sins of the world, then we have no reason to doubt his love. If he has promised to come back for us, then we have to know that he has our best interests in mind! And if your students can ever capture the magnitude of building the foundation of their faith on Jesus Christ, then you are securing them to an immovable object.

If our students' faith and hope rest on anything other than the person of Jesus Christ, they are building their lives upon fragile foundations. Eventually, the choices of life will sway them to change what they believe. Eventually, the circumstances of life will cause them to doubt God. God never intended our faith to rest upon what's going on around us.

A student's faith cannot rest on his ability to figure out the mysteries of life. Her faith cannot rest on her ability to figure out how everything fits together. A student's faith cannot rest on how consistently things go his way. The faith of a teenager cannot rest on how closely God follows her plan for her life. Her faith cannot even rest on whether or not God answers her prayers.

The foundation of our students' faith must be the person of Jesus Christ. And it is our responsibility to lead them to this conclusion.

Faith Undefined

Faith is a very simple concept to grasp. The confusion lies in our unwillingness to accept faith for what it really is rather than what we want it to be. We want faith to be a power that moves God in a direction we have prescribed. We want faith to be the code that unlocks the door to God's unlimited resources—resources that we can use at our discretion. We want faith to be the way to get what we want from God.

This way of thinking is so ingrained in us that we have a difficult time taking no for an answer. We assume there is either something wrong with us or with God. I know people who have abandoned their faith altogether because God wouldn't cooperate with them. They believed God was obligated to act on their faith. When he didn't, they walked away from the whole thing.

Students need to understand that biblical faith is not a force or a power. It is not something we tap into. It is not a tool we use to get something from God. Obi Wan Kenobi ("May the force be with you") is not the leader! That sort of thinking has a dangerous bent toward New Age philosophy and holds no weight biblically.

Biblical faith is not merely confidence. Many times students confuse confidence in something with faith in God. When a basketball team bursts out of the locker room pumped about a game, any one of those players believes he is going to win the game. And if you were to ask the fans if they have faith in their team, they would shout yes! But that's not biblical faith. That is confidence. Many students think that if they muster up enough confidence, God will do something. But again, faith is not the same as confidence.

Faith Defined

The Bible very clearly states what faith is. The writer of Hebrews says that *"faith is being sure of what we hope for and certain of what we do not see"* (11:1). Faith, then, is hope taken one step further. Hope wants something to be that is not yet, having no guarantee that it will be.

For example, if you wrote the president and invited him to visit with you and your leaders, would you have faith that he was coming? Would you announce it to your team? No. You might hope that he would honor your invitation and show up, but you wouldn't have faith that he would. What would it take for you to have faith that he was actually coming? You would need a letter or phone call confirming the fact that he had accepted your invitation. You would need a promise from him that he would be there. The promise would allow you to move from hope to faith.

The bridge from hope to faith is the promises or revelation of God. Faith, then, is confidence that God is who he says he is and will do all he has promised to do. Faith is not merely confidence. It is confidence in the promises and character of God. That's it.

The writer of Hebrews gives us dozens of illustrations, and in every case, faith is grounded in a promise or revelation of God. Noah spent one hundred and forty years building an ark because God promised that it was going to rain. Abraham left his home and set out without a destination in mind because God promised to lead him to a new home. Gideon charged down into an enemy camp totally outnumbered because God promised victory. Moses went back to Egypt after being chased out because God promised to deliver Israel through him. Joshua marched around Jericho because God told him to.

Again, faith is confidence that God is who he says he is and that he will do what he has promised to do. Walking by faith is behaving as if God is who he says he is and will do what he says he will do. It is living as if God is trustworthy.

Don't Resist

From time to time, I run into believers who resist this definition of faith. We all seem to want a faith that puts *us* in control. I wrestled with this as a high school student. I was always trying to find a way, a gimmick, or a magic prayer that would force God to do my bidding. But biblical faith leaves God firmly in control. Authentic faith leaves him with the option to say no.

Our students need to understand this distinction. For it is only when they come to terms with the true nature of faith that they will be able to surrender their wills to God's. The outcome of authentic faith is a life that is in alignment with the will of the Father. As long as our students are trying to get something *from* God, they will have a difficult time surrendering their lives *to* God.

The Good Father

In light of all that has been said thus far, one of the greatest things we can do for our students is to consistently present God as a perfect father. As my friend Louie Giglio is fond of saying, "God is not a reflection of our earthly fathers; he is the perfection of our fathers." As a perfect father, he would not dare give his children everything they ask for. Furthermore, as a perfect father, he can be trusted even when he seems to act out of character.

Jesus instructed us to address God as Father. He could have chosen any of a dozen Old Testament analogies. But he chose to address God as Father. This is how we must present him to our students. It is the only paradigm that is consistent with biblical faith.

Because he is our Father, we can ask of him anything we desire. Jesus assures us that he loves to give good gifts to his children who ask. Jesus illustrated this repeatedly in the Gospels by healing the blind and the lame, then admonishing those he healed not to tell what had happened to them. It appears Jesus healed these people just because he enjoys giving good things to those he loves. Jesus had no personal agenda. His gifts were not a means to an end. He gave because he enjoyed giving. And he continues to do so.

Promises, Promises

We have said that God can be trusted to do all he has promised to do. In teaching our students about faith, we must also teach them what God has and has not promised.

Early in this checkpoint, we noted that tragedy is often behind the demise of a student's faith. This often stems from unmet expectations. Jane prays that God will not let her parents divorce. As she prays, her expectations increase. As her expectations increase, her "faith" increases. Then Dad walks in and announces that Mom has filed for divorce.

Jane is devastated. *What's the point in praying?* she wonders. "Where is God?" she asks. "Why would he let me down like this?"

As student ministers, we face these and similar situations all the time. And there are no easy answers. Actually, there are no answers at all in the moments following a blow like that. But a proper understanding of what faith is provides a safe context for life's disappointments.

The last thing Jane needs to feel in a moment like that is isolated from God. This is when she needs to cling to him more than ever. Yet her expectations and her "faith" have set her up for disappointment with God. And as a result, she feels like she must handle her disappointment alone, without God.

Wish Lists

There are many things God has not promised that we wish he had. We must teach our students to distinguish between his promises and their expectations. God has not promised to keep bad things from happening. God has not promised to heal every illness. He has not promised to reverse the consequences of sin. Yet, there are occasions when God intervenes and does all of those things. Why? Because he is a good God who loves to give good gifts to his children.

But these are not promises. He is under no obligation. And the fact that parents divorce, grandparents die, and friends move away is no reflection on the goodness or presence of our Father.

One of the best ways to help students make these distinctions is to point them to the experiences of the apostles. These were certainly men of great faith. Yet their lives were not free from difficulty. God didn't always intervene. But their unanswered prayers did not decay their faith. For they under-stood that the foundation of their faith was not answered prayer nor their ability to interpret what God was up to. Their faith was grounded in a risen Savior.

The Promise

So what can students expect from God? What has he promised? Again, the writer of Hebrews helps us out. He sheds some light on two things we can always expect from our heavenly Father. See if you can spot them.

> Therefore, since we have a great high priest who has gone through the heavens, Jesus the Son of God, let us hold firmly to the faith we profess. For we do not have a high priest who is unable to sympathize with our weak-nesses, but we have one who has been tempted in every way, just as we are—yet was without sin. Let us then ap-proach the throne of grace with confidence, so that we may receive mercy and find grace to help us in our time of need. *(Hebrews 4:14–16)*

We can continue believing because we have a high priest who has, on his own merit, *"gone through the heavens."* A high priest who can sympathize with our weaknesses and tempta-tions. With all that as a backdrop, the writer invites us to *"ap-proach the throne of grace with confidence."*

"Confidence in what?" you ask. "He may not give me what I want. He may say no."

We can approach God's throne with confidence that he will always give us the two things that are most critical in our time of need: mercy and grace.

Mercy

Mercy comes in many forms. Sometimes it is simply the comfort of knowing that in some mysterious way we have God's undivided attention when we pour our hearts out to him. At times, mercy comes in the form of physical or emotional relief. Mercy is the assurance that God will never allow the pressures or heartbreaks of life to be more than we can bear.

When I taught this principle to our students, I assured them that their Savior knew far more of what they were experiencing than they imagined. Then I took them on a journey through Christ's experiences. My goal was to help them see that he is capable of entering into their pain even when he chooses to do nothing about it.

Here are some highlights from that study:

✓ Fear . . . He spent a night dreading the events of the next day.

✓ Rejection . . . He experienced the rejection of his friends and family members.

✓ **Failure** . . . He experienced having everything he lived for crumble around him.

✓ **Temptation** . . . He experienced temptation from Satan himself.

✓ **Loneliness** . . . He faced death alone.

✓ **Abandonment** . . . His friends ran away when he needed them most.

My point was that we have a Savior who understands. He has felt what we have felt. Therefore, he knows exactly what we need. The writer of Hebrews says that we can come to him with confidence. Students need to know they can boldly come to God with total transparency and openness. He is never going to say, "I can't believe you did that." He will never answer quizzically, "I can't believe you feel that way." He will never ask emphatically, "What is your problem?" He is the mercy-giving God because he knows from experience what it is like to need mercy.

Grace

But God's promises don't end with mercy. Your students can expect to receive grace as well. In this context, grace is the strength to endure, the ability to carry on.

Your mom or stepdad may never lighten up. Dad may never come back. Mom may never understand. Popularity may always be elusive. The scholarship may never become a reality. But God has promised you the strength to endure.

God has not promised to deliver us *from* our circumstances. He has promised to deliver us *through* them. Students need to know that they have the freedom to ask God to change their circumstances. And they can count on him for the grace to endure in the meantime.

Saving Faith

When I was a kid, I must have asked Jesus to come into my heart a thousand times. I just wanted to make sure. I thought salvation was like a bad cold. I wanted to make sure I "got it."

I remember evangelists preaching about "head faith" versus "heart faith." Head faith, they said, wasn't enough. You had to believe in your heart. After all, even the devil believes in his head! So, I would pray for heart faith . . . just in case I still hadn't caught it.

I know my experience is not unique. I talk to students all the time who have "prayed the prayer" a dozen times and still aren't sure if they are "saved." This confusion stems from a general misunderstanding about the nature of faith. Somewhere along the way, we got the notion that the "quality" of our faith is an issue with God. So, students pray for salvation and wonder if they "really" believed or believed "enough" or believed "in their hearts." Combine that with the emphasis we have put on "praying the prayer," and it is no wonder the same kids get "saved" year after year.

In light of what we have said about faith in general, saving faith should be easy to explain and understand. God has promised to forgive our sins, once and for all, if we put our faith in Christ's death as the payment for our sin. That's the gospel. Saving faith is simply a matter of trusting in Christ's death as the payment for sin.

When students come to me, doubting their salvation, I don't ask them if they have prayed to receive Christ. I ask them what they are trusting in to get them to heaven. Just about every time I have asked students that question, they have said, "I am trusting in Jesus." To which I respond, "Then you are in!"

Having said it simply, let me try to confuse you with more information.

The Facts About Faith

Faith must always have an object. If I told you that I was going to visit you, the object of your faith would be me. The object of faith is usually a person or a product. The object of faith is *whom* you believe.

Faith must always have content as well. When you believe in a product, you believe something about the product. The content of faith is what a person or product promises to do for you. The content of faith is what you believe.

Saving faith has a very specific object and a very specific content. The object of saving faith is Jesus, not just God. Jesus said, *"I am the way and the truth and the life. No one comes to the Father except through me"* (John 14:6).

But what, specifically, does a student need to believe about Jesus? The content of saving faith lies in two concrete stakes that must be driven deep in the hearts of your students: Jesus is the Son of God, and his death on the cross paid for all our sin, apart from anything we do or intend to do.

Students can believe a multitude of other things about Christ. They can believe Jesus was born of a virgin, did miracles, died on a cross, and never sinned, but these are not the critical elements of saving faith. The problem with saving faith is not that it is so complex, but that it is so simple.

We are saved by faith. The way by which a person comes to salvation is faith. If you ask a student next Sunday morning why he's at church, he would not answer "because of my car!" His car did not guarantee his presence. His car is the vehicle that got him to church. It is not the reason he's there. Faith is the vehicle that carries a student to salvation. We are saved *through* faith, but not *because of* faith.

Salvation is a gift from God. This is not a reward. God does not offer it because we deserve it. God offers every person salvation because that is his desire. The way a student receives that gift of salvation is through trusting in God's offer. That is saving faith. It is confidence that God is who he says he is and that he will do what he has promised to do.

Faith and Direction

There is a promise attached to authentic faith. The writer of Proverbs describes it this way:

> Trust in the LORD with all your heart and lean not on your own understanding; in all your ways submit to him, and he will make your paths straight. *(Proverbs 3:5–6 TNIV)*

The challenge in this verse is one we need to bring to our students repeatedly. Trust in the Lord with all your heart. That is, trust the Lord with every area of your life. He is a perfect father who can be trusted.

Notice the promise. In response to our trust/faith, he promises guidance. Literally, God will make our paths clear and obvious. I love what Thomas Merton said in this regard:

> We receive enlightenment only in proportion as we give ourselves more completely to God by humble submission and love. We do not first see, and then act: we act, then see . . . and that is why the man who waits to see clearly before he will believe never starts on the journey. *(Ascent to Truth)*

If our students are going to trust in the Lord with "all" of their hearts, they must be assured that God is trustworthy. We need to do everything in our power to provide them with the proper context for making that determination. It is up to us to remove the fog surrounding the issue of faith and to assure them that God is who he says he is, a perfect father. And like a perfect father, he will do everything he has promised to do— and more.

Checking In
Checkpoint: Authentic Faith

Bible Study Assignment

✓ Read the first four chapters of Hebrews.

✓ Read Hebrews 11:1.

Questions:

✓ Have you ever changed the way you believed about something? By that I mean you decided there was nothing wrong with what you were doing and changed the way you believed about it. _____

_____

_____

_____

✓ Has tragedy caused you to doubt or lose faith in God? Explain. _____

_____

_____

_____

✓ In your own words, define faith (use Hebrews 11:1 as your guide). _____

_____

_____

_____

✓ Read Hebrews 4:14. Would you say you hold firmly to your faith? Why or why not? _____

_____

_____

_____

✓ Read Hebrews 1–3 and make a list of evidence that Jesus is God. _____

_____

_____

_____

✓ What does this evidence mean to you? _____

_____

_____

_____

✓ In general, is the faith of your students more circumstance focused than Christ focused? Why or why not?

_____

_____

_____

Checkpoint #2
Spiritual Disciplines

IF I CAN SEE AS GOD SEES,
I WILL DO AS GOD SAYS

If you want to be somebody else,

if you're tired of losing battles with yourself,

if you want to be somebody else . . .

change your mind.

—Sister Hazel, *Change Your Mind*

Checkpoint
Spiritual Disciplines

Critical Question
Are your students developing a consistent devotional and prayer
life?

Principle
If I can see as God sees, I will do as God says.

Key Passage
Romans 12:2

Spiritual Disciplines
DILEMMA

In the days of Christopher Columbus, the common belief was that the world was flat; if you sailed to the horizon, you would fall off the earth to your death. Columbus was contemplating this belief one day while sitting under a tree eating an orange. A butterfly landed on top of the orange, and Columbus watched in wonder as the butterfly walked down the backside of the orange without falling off. Columbus reasoned that the same force of nature (gravity) that kept the butterfly connected to his orange would keep him and his ship connected to the earth. His perspective changed. Consequently, Columbus sailed past the horizon and discovered what we now call home.

It's true. The way we perceive things shapes our reality. This principle could explain why students do most of the things they do. From faith issues to selfishness, it is perspective that drives a student's behavior.

With that in mind, our calling as student leaders is very simple. We are to do everything in our power to help our students see as God sees. If they can gain God's perspective, they are more apt to do what he says. Simple? Yes. Easy? No.

The Big "D"

The good news is that God has documented his take on all of life—in the Scriptures. The bad news is that our students look to us to chop it up and feed it to them in bite-size morsels. It is the discipline of reading God's Word, understanding what it means, and doing what it says that students struggle with. For the most part, discipline and teenager are mutually exclusive concepts.

After all, aren't the teenage years designed for the sole purpose of irresponsibility? Parents and student leaders accept irresponsible behavior from students. It is what we have come to expect.

Unfortunately, we lower our expectations for students in their spiritual disciplines as well. The ability of teenagers to develop consistent spiritual disciplines will have a dramatic impact on the quality of their relationship with Christ.

A Changed Life

Most teenagers would agree that becoming a Christian means their lives should change. When there are no immediate or consistent differences, they begin to wonder about the reality of their faith. Many students, as well as adults, assume that "praying the prayer" or making a commitment at the end of a church service or camp should automatically result in lasting change. But, as you know, the Christian life doesn't work that way. Prayer is not a magic bullet that guarantees change. And rededication is nothing more than a promise. It does not ensure the ability to follow through.

The apostle Paul put a different spin on change when he wrote:

Do not conform any longer to the pattern of this world, but be transformed by the renewing of your mind. *(Romans 12:2)*

So what does bring about transformation or change? A renewed mind. But renewal is not instantaneous. Renewal is a process of taking off old things and putting on new things. In the context of life in Christ, renewal is the process of removing lies and replacing them with truth.

Ask yourself: when students give their lives to Christ, does God erase the lustful thoughts and insecurities that have harassed those students throughout their lives? No. Those students wake up the next morning fighting the same things they battled the day before. Their identities will be in Christ, but their minds will still be full of crud.

Your students will never live transformed lives until they have transformed minds. And they will never have transformed minds until they have God's thoughts. It is his perspective, his mind that students need to gain. And your students will never gain God's thoughts until they exercise the spiritual disciplines of time alone with God, Scripture memory, journaling, and prayer. In addition, Paul's statement on renewal in Romans must become foremost in our minds as student leaders if we want to see life change happen.

Listen Up!

Students always find the time to tell God what they need done or fixed. But how much time do they give him to speak? I have never met a student whose problems stemmed from the fact that he didn't talk enough to God. I have talked to numerous students whose problems stemmed from the fact that they never developed the habit of listening to God. Most students' major regrets could have been avoided if they had obeyed God. Communication is a key component to intimacy, and communication involves listening.

Jesus understood this. Nowhere do we see the importance of communication with the Father better illustrated than in the life of Jesus. In fact, Jesus' time alone with the Father was his ultimate priority. It took priority over ministry, family, friends, and even sleep. In spite of all he had to do, Jesus made time to be with his Father (see Luke 5:15–16). He refused to allow the expectations of others shape his agenda. As strange as it sounds, he put his own spiritual welfare ahead of the spiritual and physical welfare of others.

Jesus came to do the will of the Father. In order to do the

will of the Father, he had to know the will of the Father. Jesus made it a priority to know the One who sent him.

Time alone with God must become our students' priority as well, if they are serious about pursuing intimacy with God. God wants to communicate to your students and not just do things for them. God will speak to them through his Word in a real way when given opportunities to do so.

So why don't they spend time with God? Many students argue that they didn't realize they were supposed to. Other students say they don't know how to spend time with God. But the main reason that students don't spend time alone with God is that it isn't urgent.

Urgency

Getting to school, practice, or work on time is urgent. Homework may even fall into the urgent category. But time alone with God doesn't generally get the same status as these other "important" activities. After all, if they miss a quiet time or two (or twenty), there are no immediate consequences. They aren't kicked off the team. They don't have to take a class over. Nobody sends a letter to their parents.

When students don't set aside time to listen to God, however, eventually they pay a price. If they don't listen, they won't learn. If they don't learn, they won't change. They won't show proper respect for God. They will approach him like a vending machine with "give me, bless me, help me" attitudes. If students don't listen to God, what began as a relationship will devolve into a routine, a ritual, a religion.

Find the Time

Obviously, God can speak to your students whenever and wherever he wishes. By helping students develop a scheduled time alone with God, we are not advocating putting God in a box. But as leaders, we must help them prioritize their lives around listening to God. A daily time alone with him postures students to listen. Time alone with God develops in a teenager a listening heart.

We need to help students choose a place to listen. It could be a guestroom, a corner of a bedroom, or a particular chair in the living room. When I was in high school, I would drive to a park before school and sit on a certain rock.

When I need to tell my wife something important, I avoid certain environments. The dinner table is one. Loud restaurants are never good. If you come to see me about something important, you won't want to sit and talk to me in the lobby of our offices. There are too many distractions. Jesus knew this, and that is why he went up into the mountains, to the wilderness, or to a garden. He left the disciples so that he could be alone with his Father.

In addition to the proper place, students need to choose

a proper time. If I want to talk to my wife about something important, it needs to be before 10:30 p.m. Jesus often slipped away early in the morning. That was the optimal listening time for him.

Students make dates for everything else in their cluttered lives. Choosing a time for God can become the priority in their days as well. Challenge students to schedule their times with God. They need to go to bed knowing when and where they will meet with him the next day. The reason students don't spend time alone with God is because they don't *plan* to. If they wanted to spend some time with you, they would schedule it. The "let's get together" thing rarely works. Students need to think of these times as their appointments with God.

All By Myself

Think about these names:

- ✓ Abraham

- ✓ Moses

- ✓ Joshua

- ✓ Jonah

- ✓ David

- ✓ John the Baptist

✓ Paul

✓ Jesus

All of these men have a common thread in their histories: God allowed them to go through an extended time of solitude before they began to influence the world. We often look at their solitudes as times of punishment. But God looked at their solitudes as environments for transformation. God still looks at solitude the same way.

Jesus considered solitude important:

> **Very early in the morning, while it was still dark, Jesus got up, left the house and went off to a solitary place, where he prayed. Simon and his companions went to look for him, and when they found him, they exclaimed, "Everyone is looking for you!"** *(Mark 1:35–37)*

Verse 35 starts with ten words that most of us detest:

> **Very early in the morning, while it was still dark**

I personally think that early morning is the best time for students to spend time with God. It is a practical way of applying *"Seek first his kingdom and his righteousness"* (Matthew 6:33).

Jesus modeled solitude with the Father. It serves to mentally and morally reboot a student's conscience and perspective. It clears out previous confusion. It ensures that nothing will interrupt. It is first. It allows students to pray through their schedules for the day. If your students are anything like mine, they will argue that they are not "morning people." But the truth is they will do *something* first every morning.

My Place

If Jesus sought solitude, our students should certainly pursue it as well. All of us have played hide and seek. Think about those hiding places where no one could find you. Remember hearing your own heart beat while you waited for someone to walk by? Remember listening to yourself breathe? Remember that you didn't dare move for fear of being found? Your environment of solitude created all of that. You didn't want to be found . . . neither did Jesus.

Now What?

Why did Jesus get up early in the morning, while it was still dark, leave the house, and go off to a solitary place? Verse 35 concludes with these three words: *where he prayed*. Solitude will always seem like a waste of time if there is no purpose in it. Solitude with purpose breeds discipline. Solitude without purpose can result in isolation. Jesus had a reason to be alone: intimacy with his Father.

The Why Behind the What

Scripture enables students to see things as God sees them, which in turn clarifies what they should do and why he asks them to do it. In Scripture, students discover the *why* behind the *what*. Your students have been taught things like "sex before marriage is wrong" and "honor your mother and father." Scripture tells them why they should obey the what.

Students resist the truths of Scripture because they don't see as God sees. It makes no sense to them. As a parent I find myself wanting to make decisions for my kids. The root of this is my desire for them to see things the way I do so they will do what I say. One day my son and I went shopping for a Mother's Day gift, and every parent's nightmare became my reality. As I became engrossed in what I wanted to get my wife, my son wandered off. Not seeing him, I frantically called his name and searched under the racks of clothes. I happened to look up and see a man repeatedly bending over about three aisles down. I rushed over to see if my son was involved. To my dismay, this "man" was actually a mannequin. My son was pulling the mannequin by the hands while he danced and sang "Get jiggy with it!" The mannequin was just about to come off its stand and onto my son. As you would expect, I rushed over and rescued him from his new friend. Then I explained why dancing with a mannequin was not the safest recreation in the world. He did not understand. He cried and cried because he wanted to dance with the mannequin. He didn't see things the way I saw them, and he didn't want to do what I said.

God's Value System

Scripture enables students to see what's important to God and why. Scripture reveals God's value system. Scripture enables students to see the condition of their hearts. God designed Scripture to play an active role in our lives. The Bible is more than good literature. If students allow them, the Scriptures will serve as an active tool to reveal the true condition of their hearts—their prejudices and their attitudes. The writer of Hebrews illustrates this: *"The word of God is living and active. Sharper than any double-edged sword, it penetrates even to dividing soul and spirit, joints and marrow; it judges the thoughts and attitudes of the heart"* (4:12).

God speaks to the core issues of a student's life through the Scriptures. Scripture is where students find out how deeply they are loved. Scripture has the power to root out the anger behind the depression of this generation of students. It has the power to root out the insecurity behind your students' self-destructive habits. Scripture is where your students can be overwhelmed with the price God paid to know them and to be known by them.

Students have the biggest decisions of life ahead of them. They need to see as God sees as it relates to singleness, sex, and marriage. If they can begin to see as God sees now, they will be much more inclined to do as he says when the time comes. Teenagers need to see as God sees as it relates to friends. They will discover that their friends will determine the quality and direction of their lives. That is a whole lot easier to take from God than from their moms and dads.

Intimacy requires communication. Communication involves listening. God is willing to speak to your students through his Word—if they will listen.

What students do during their time with God can vary. I personally think that many students allow the routine to rob them of the intimacy and the wonder that should characterize a relationship with our Creator. Using a quiet-time book like *The Seven Checkpoints Student Journal*, listening to a CD, or finding a beautiful spot outside to sit in silence are all great things. God loves variety.

The Big Four

There are four components, however, that students need to incorporate into their time alone with God. The first is reading the Word of God. Much has been made about how long a student should meet with God and what to do during that time. The real issue is neither of those things, but rather what the student will walk away with. And if the goal is renewing their minds for change, then the Word of God must be central to that process.

Students can read as much or as little as they want. What they need to develop more than anything else is the habit of answering four questions as they work their way through the Scriptures:

✓ **What does this passage say?**
  What does this mean to me in my own words?

✓ **Why is this important?**
  Why do I need to know this?

✓ **What should I do about it?**
  How can I apply this to my life today?

✓ **How can I remember this?**
  What's the best way for me to remember this verse?
  (Write it on a card, ask for accountability, etc.)

We Have to Pray!

A second major component of their time with God is prayer. Help students pray in concentric circles of concern, beginning with what is closest to their hearts, and moving toward those things that are of less concern. Here's an easy way to help them know what to pray for:

Pray through the passage they just read.
  ✓ Lord, help me to be like the person I just read
  about . . .

✓ Lord, when I face a trial, remind me that it is a test
of my faith . . .

✓ Lord, help me to forgive as you have forgiven me . . .

Pray through their day.

✓ Today, I will be tempted to . . .

✓ Today, I am meeting with . . .

✓ Today, when he or she approaches me, . . .

Pray through their relationships.

✓ Family

✓ Friends

✓ Acquaintances

Write On!

The third major component of our students' time with God
is journaling. A journal is simply a personal, written record of
what God is teaching them and what he is doing in their lives.
Its purpose is to record their spiritual journeys. Students will
write things in their journals—like how they're feeling at a
certain point in time—that they normally would not express
anywhere else or in any other way.

This can be very healthy and freeing, especially during the tumultuous teenage years, when emotions can be particularly difficult to process.

I have found that for students, journaling is probably better practiced as a weekly discipline rather than a daily one. But it is still important. Looking back is the only way for students to see how far they have come. I started journaling when I was seventeen years old. Now, whenever I get discouraged or think God has walked away, a quick review of my journal is all I need to remind me that God is faithful and vitally active in my life. Students need to be able to do this in their lives too.

Memories . . .

The fourth component to a strong devotional life is Scripture memorization. Unlike Bible study, prayer, and journaling, Scripture memory is something that can be (probably should be) done outside the confines of their scheduled solitude. Scripture memory and meditation are ways of extending their devotional lives beyond their scheduled quiet times.

Why is Scripture memory so important? With more information at our fingertips than at any other time in history, it would seem like we would have better things to do than fill our minds with more "stuff." "Besides," students may reason, "God left us the Bible. We have it at our disposal at any time. Any problem I have can be answered when I get home or go to church on Sunday. There is no need for me to remember what God says, because most of the Bible doesn't relate to my everyday teenage life. What I need to remember is how to do calculus and trigonometry!"

For those students who have not grown up in church, the need to remember God's Word seems like another religious thing to do. For those students who have, Scripture memory has always seemed like some sort of competition that has never connected with who they really are and what they deal with as teenagers. They may have memorized a bunch of verses, but they have no idea what they mean and how they relate.

So why memorize God's Word?

The truth is that the mind of a student will be his or her greatest strength or greatest downfall. Students do the things they do because of the way they think. How you act is a direct result of how you think. Teenagers' actions are simply live portraits, or movies, of their thoughts.

✓ If students tend to be concerned about clothes and how they look, there is a good chance they base their self-worth on how good or bad they look.

✓ If the person a student is dating is aggressive physically, there is a good chance he or she thinks of that student as an object and of sex as the basis of love.

✓ If a teenage guy tends to overreact when he fails, there is a pretty good chance he thinks his significance is based on success.

✓ Teenagers who work hard all the time probably think their significance is based on money and/or material things.

Consequently, your ministry is full of teenagers who are not exactly excited about the movie playing in their "theaters."

Raw Sewage

Culture and society have polluted the minds of your students with lies since they were born. Think about the progression of knowledge *you* went through:

✓ When and how was the first time you learned what cuss words were?

✓ When and how did you first belittle someone?

✓ When and how did you first think of yourself before others?

✓ When and how did you first learn about your sexuality?

The minds of our students have been slowly but surely polluted with sin and lies. Much of this pollution comes from the loss of innocence. Gradually and without warning, students begin to contribute to this pollution.

Paul illustrated this in his letter to the church in Rome by writing, *"They (humankind) have become filled with every kind of wickedness, evil, greed and depravity. They are full of envy, murder, strife, deceit and malice. They are gossips, slanderers, God-haters, insolent, arrogant and boastful; they invent ways of doing evil; they disobey their parents; they are senseless, faithless, heartless, ruthless"* (1:29–31). Does that remotely sound like any student you know? What is more telling is that these words describe some of the sharpest teenagers in your ministry!

Consequently, all of your students exhibit a living cinema of what they believe. Their minds are the scripts; their lives are the live screenplays. Jesus described this by saying,

What comes out of a man is what makes him "unclean." For from within, out of men's hearts, come evil thoughts, sexual immorality, theft, murder, adultery, greed, malice, deceit, lewdness, envy, slander, arrogance and folly. All these evils come from inside and make a man "unclean." *(Mark 7:20–23)*

Edit the Script

The only way your teenagers will change the dramas of their lives is by changing their scripts. Most students think that Christianity is about changing their behavior. As we have said several times, their behavior won't change until they change their belief systems. Scripture memorization is rewriting the script to change the movie. Scripture memory is replacing the lies a student believes and acts on with the truth. Students have to develop the discipline of replacing the lies with the truth.

Is it any wonder you have teenagers who have made some type of commitment to God, yet their lives never attest to that fact? Why? Because the way a student thinks determines how he acts. A student's belief system determines her behavior. Your students act the way they do because of the way they think. The truth is that we have a tendency to be spiritually dyslexic in student ministry. When students ask Jesus to save them, Christ changes their identities. The Spirit of God takes up residence inside of those students. However, he doesn't change their minds.

Irish Spring

If your mom was anything like mine, you may have the distinct memory of having your mouth washed out with soap. I can still remember the inappropriate term that landed me in our avocado green bathroom. My bicycle had fallen in the driveway, and I said, "Get that darn bicycle out of my way." Little did I know that mom had just stepped out on the front porch. Funny how moms always appeared at just the right and wrong times. I'm not sure what the theory is behind washing a child's mouth out with soap. But in my case, it was very effective.

Scripture memory, in essence, is the discipline of consistently and purposely washing our *minds* out with the "soap" of truth, or God's Word. The difference? The Bible has no bad aftertaste!

Occasional Truth

Scripture memorization must be consistent. We tend to connect repetition with boring. But repetition is a key to learning.

- ✓ How did you learn to drive?

- ✓ How did you learn math and English?

- ✓ How did you learn to ski or ride a bike?

- ✓ How did you learn to shoot a basketball?

Memorizing Scripture will not have its desired effect if it is not practiced on a regular basis. Reading a verse is not memorizing it. And knowing a verse by heart is not even the issue. At the heart of this discipline is students consistently washing their minds out with the soap of God's Word. A great illustration of renewal is girls and fingernail polish. When a girl wants to put on new polish, she doesn't paint over the old! She dabs this unbelievably stinky potion on a cotton swab and removes the old polish. She then applies the new polish to her nails. Eventually the new will become old, and the process will start all over again. That's renewal!

Intentional Truth

Scripture memory must also be *intentional* and *purposeful*. There is nothing worse than trying to learn something that seemingly has no value or application. Students feel that way when they have to take algebra and trigonometry or climb a rope in gym class. Scripture memory can become meaningless to your students if they are doing it randomly. Memorizing Leviticus 2:2 really has no significance. All Scripture is inspired, but not all of it is applicable to a teenager! We need to point students to the verses that are particularly applicable to their particular stage of life.

Stuart told me this story and I think it illustrates this principle:

When I was growing up in lowly Wilmer, Alabama, home of the world-famous speed trap and now the West Alabama Zoo (I am not joking), we had a huge pear tree in our backyard. The ground under the tree would be covered with pears every year. This was cool until I had to cut the grass. Because my brother and I were too lazy to pick up the gazillion pears on the ground, we would simply run over them with the lawnmower. And, of course, one of two things would happen: either the blade of the mower would get messed up, leaving the mower useless, or the pears would shoot out from under the mower like missiles. May I just say that being hit by a pear going fifty miles an hour hurts!

One day, out of total frustration with my brother and me, my dad told me to handle the problem with the pear tree (expletives not included). In disgust, I walked out to the tree with a bucket and proceeded to pick all the pears off the ground and the tree. I walked back inside with a bucketful of pears, and in my mind, the mission was complete. My dad proceeded to share with me that I had dealt with the fruit of the tree, but if I never wanted to deal with it again, I should dig the tree up by its *roots*.

Novel idea, I thought.

Memorizing Scripture is very much like this. If your students are going to have transformed lives, then dealing with the fruit of their thinking is futile at best. The task is to replace the lies they have allowed to infiltrate their minds with the truth of God's Word. They must get to the root of the problem.

The Lie Detector

But how does a student identify the lies?

The apostle Paul wrote:

Though we live in the world, we do not wage war as the world does. The weapons we fight with are not the weapons of the world. On the contrary, they have divine power to demolish strongholds. We demolish arguments and every pretension that sets itself up against the knowledge of God, and we take captive every thought to make it obedient to Christ. *(2 Corinthians 10:3–5)*

Paul implies that these lies become places for the Enemy to fortify himself for his fight against us. Paul calls these places "strongholds." A stronghold is anything that exalts itself in our minds. A stronghold appears to be more powerful than God. It steals our focus and causes us to feel controlled or mastered.

How can your students know if they have strongholds in their lives?

✓ What steals their focus?

✓ What controls their thinking?

✓ What or who is the master of their lives?

Identifying strongholds is as simple as determining what consumes their thoughts and steals their focus from the truth.

Tear Them Down!

Once students identify their strongholds, they can choose the verses that combat those strongholds and memorize them. Being intentional about Scripture memory makes the process useful and not some futile spiritual exercise. I strongly encourage our students to make truth visible. Having a note card with a memory verse on it means they can have truth visible at meals, while watching television, or talking on the phone. They can put the verse cards on their rearview mirrors or dashboards. They can have them by their beds, on the ceilings above their beds, or on their bathroom mirrors. I know students who have even written verses on the undersides of their baseball-hat brims. All of these help them think about how the verses relate to them and how they can act on these truths.

Top Shelf Truth

Finally, Scripture memory must become a priority in our students' lives for it to work. Half-hearted Scripture memory will never change a life. Taking the time and energy to memorize God's Word, understand his Word, and wash their minds with it consistently are what make the change. The priority this takes will be determined by how badly students desire to be people of truth.

✓ Their characters lie in this discipline.

✓ Their integrity lies in this discipline.

✓ Their desire to serve others lies in this discipline.

How can a young man (or woman) keep his way pure? By living according to your word. I seek you with all my heart; do not let me stray from your commands. I have hidden your word in my heart that I might not sin against you. *(Psalm 119:9–11)*

The point is simple. We remember things that are important to us: phone numbers, passwords, addresses, websites, birthdays, anniversaries, what we wore to school last week, our favorite menus and prices, measurements, songs. The list could go on and on.

Memorization, defined by Webster, is to commit something to memory or learn by heart. *Memory*, defined by Webster, is the power or process of reproducing or recalling what has been learned and retained through associative mechanisms. Webster also defines memory as "evidenced by modification of structure or behavior . . ."

The reason students memorize Scripture is so that they will react to life's struggles, tensions, and trials by acting on truth. A mind full of truth will result in a life exemplified by truth. If students see as God sees, they will do as God says.

Be Strong and Take Heart

Here's a touching story Stuart told me that illustrates this truth . . .

October of 2000 will always serve as a lesson on perspective for me. Our five-year-old son, Grant, had been experiencing bleeding from his rectum and in his stool. Contrary to our regular pediatrician's diagnosis, our visit to a specialist confirmed the seriousness of the matter. We were told that the problem could be anything from a polyp to leukemia and that Grant would need immediate surgery to determine what the problem actually was. When cancer was mentioned, my heart sank and fear ravished my mind and soul.

I immediately asked God for some kind of promise. I needed his perspective so I could act accordingly. I landed on Psalm 31:24, a verse I had taught to our students two weeks earlier. It says "Be strong, and take heart all who hope in the LORD." I wrote that verse down for my wife and began to teach Grant the verse too. Fear was evident in Grant's life as well. When I picked him up from school for his preop tests, his first words to me were, "Daddy, I'm scared." My response to him—Psalm 31:24.

On the day of Grant's surgery, he was given a drug to make him drowsy. His speech became slurred, and it was very comical to watch him battle cows flying at him and clouds moving in the room. Just before they rolled him back to surgery, we prayed together. When I was done praying, I could hear him whispering something under his breath. I leaned down to hear what he was saying. He was saying Psalm 31:24. He was attacking fear with truth! He was seeing things as God sees them and doing what he says.

Relationship Versus Religion

A strong devotional life will do more to transition your students from a religious approach to God to a relational one than anything else. If there is no intimate communication, God is relegated to buildings and days of the week. He becomes a duty. This accounts for students who go to church every week but whose everyday lives aren't changed. This may be the very reason that so many students, when they graduate from high school, never darken the doors of church again. A strong devotional life is what develops a sense of accountability between your students and their Father. When students develop the habit of spending personal time alone with God, they enter into a new realm of accountability. All the difference in the world lies between hearing something convicting and sitting alone with God's Word and hearing from him.

Checking In
Checkpoint: Spiritual Disciplines

Bible Study Assignment

✓ Read Deuteronomy 6:1–11 and Moses' instruction to the people of Israel.

✓ Read Psalm 119.

Questions:

✓ Journal your thoughts on this statement:

"Solitude is the furnace for transformation."

(Henri Nouwen)

_____

_____

_____

✓ How did God use solitude in the lives of each of these men?

What was their solitude?

1. Abraham

2. Moses

3. Joshua

4. Jonah

5. David

6. John the Baptist

7. Jesus

✓ How do you develop spiritual disciplines in the lives of your students? _____

_____

_____

_____

✓ In your opinion, what is the greatest enemy of students developing spiritual disciplines?_____

_____

_____

_____

✓ Do you consider God's Word an intimate part of your life? Why or why not? _____

_____

_____

_____

✓ In what area(s) do you need God's perspective in your own life and ministry?_____

_____

_____

_____

✓ If you were to title the movie of your life today, what would it be and why (determined by the things you have done consistently in your life)? _____

_____

_____

_____

Checkpoint #3
Moral Boundaries
PAVING THE WAY FOR INTIMACY

And the way young people talk about sex.
Sex is awesome, yeah, but in the right context.
—David Robinson, *ESPN the Magazine*
(when asked what he deplored most in people)

Checkpoint
Moral Boundaries

Critical Question
Are your students establishing and maintaining moral
boundaries?

Principle
Paving the Way for Intimacy

Key Passage
1 Thessalonians 4:3–8

Moral Boundaries
DILEMMA

I take every opportunity I get to remind students that God created sex. We don't know how the idea occurred to him. But we do know that a long time ago, in a galaxy far, far away, there was no sex. Then one day God said to himself, or perhaps aloud, "I've got a great idea!"

Okay, so maybe my imagination has moved beyond the boundaries of what is reverent. But the fact remains: sex is a creation. It was God's idea. So, it is safe to assume that he knows more about the subject than any of us. "Us" would include Kanye, Hugh, Paris, and any of the assorted television and radio hosts that pollute the airways with their misinformation.

Sex can be unbelievably fulfilling (and fun). And sex can leave a man or a woman feeling used and empty. Which do you suppose God prefers? Unless sex is for procreation only, I think it is safe to assume that God wants our sexual experiences to be fulfilling (and fun). So next week, when you are making announcements in church, go ahead and praise God out loud for the wonderful gift of sex. Don't hold back. Say something along the lines of, "This is the day that the Lord has made. And I'm grateful for sex as well, aren't you? God is so good!"

My point? My point is that God wants us to experience

sex in a way that fully exploits the joy and fulfillment that this wonderful gift has to offer. He wants our sexual experiences to be the best they can possibly be. As I tell our students, God has created you with the potential to experience great sex. Way to go, God!

That's Different

I'm not sure that is the message the church has communicated to our students. In fact, the whole notion that God is interested in the quality of their sex lives would cause even the most callous students to do a double take. I imagine it might have caused you some slight discomfort during the past three minutes.

The message we have sent to the students in our churches is "Wait." That is translated by many of our students as just another big NO to go along with all the other NOs we have cast their way.

I think we need to change our focus. There is nothing enticing, stimulating, or motivating about "Wait." For many of our kids, "Wait" sounds like the desperate cry of a generation looking to leverage its last bit of control.

Besides, "Wait" brings an immediate outcry of "Why? Why wait?" So why not shift the focus of our message to the *why* behind the *what*? For it is there that we find a compelling reason for students to reserve sex for marriage.

"Why Wait?"

If I could drill one simple principle into the minds and hearts of students as it relates to sex, it would be this: *purity paves the way to intimacy.* When we ask kids to wait, we are really asking them to remain pure. So the questions we must answer are: "Why remain pure?" "What's the big advantage of purity?" "What do I gain by remaining pure that balances what I give up if I choose not to?"

The answer to all three questions is *intimacy.* Intimacy is the joy of knowing someone fully and being known fully without fear of rejection. Again, purity paves the way to intimacy. Impurity erodes one's capacity to experience intimacy. Consequently, impurity diminishes sexual satisfaction.

If you have ever counseled with people who have been sexually abused, you know that they often struggle with intimacy in their marriages. Why? Because there is an inexorable link between purity and intimacy. Even unwanted sexual involvement affects an individual's capacity for intimacy.

Men and women who have had affairs admit that even if they are able to hold their marriages together, they never achieve the intimacy they once had with their spouses. Impurity (in this case immorality) always affects intimacy. There is no escaping this principle.

It may be what is behind the apostle Paul's warning to the Corinthians when he writes:

Flee immorality. Every other sin that a man commits is outside the body, but the immoral man sins against his own body. *(1 Corinthians 6:18 NASB)*

Our students need to know that when they sin sexually, they hurt themselves. Furthermore, they are robbing their future spouses of intimacy as well. Perhaps this is why Paul says that sexual sin is unique.

I tell the girls in our student ministry, "You don't really want sex. What you want is intimacy. You want to meet a guy, fall in love, and know you can trust him completely. You want somebody with whom you can share everything there is to know about you without fear of betrayal or rejection. You want to be fully known and to know him fully. Purity *now* paves the way to intimacy *later.*"

I love to challenge our young men the same way. I say, "Guys, I know what you want. You want to meet a girl you are physically attracted to, fall in love with her, and never lose that physical attraction." I go on to say, "One of your greatest fears is marrying a woman and losing your attraction to her; feeling stuck." The best way for our young men to ensure that they don't lose "that loving feeling" is to set their sights on intimacy, rather than sex. Great sex is the byproduct of maximum intimacy.

I have counseled dozens of attractive couples who are no

longer attracted to each other—couples whose sex lives are nonexistent. Why? Because in spite of all they knew about sex, they knew little or nothing about intimacy. And without intimacy, the sexual part of their relationship slowly died.

More Than Physical

The reason satisfying sex and intimacy go together is because sex is not just physical, it is relational. Unfortunately, in our society, sex is almost never talked about or portrayed in the context of long-term relationships. Society has ripped sex out of its relational context. Sex is usually presented as something akin to a sporting event, an activity, or something (or someone) you *do*. For most of our students, especially our young men, sex is purely physical.

But God says sex is highly relational. And when you rip it out of its relational context, there will always be problems. There will always be consequences. It will always be less than satisfying. Look at how God described sex in the beginning.

The LORD God caused a deep sleep to fall upon the man, and he slept; then He took one of his ribs and closed up the flesh at that place. And the LORD God fashioned into a woman the rib He had taken from the man, and brought her to the man. And the man said, "This is now bone of my bones, and flesh of my flesh; she shall be called Woman, because she was taken out of Man."

For this reason a man shall leave his father and his mother, and be joined to his wife; and they shall become one flesh. *(Genesis 2:21–24 NASB)*

Sex resulted in Adam and Eve's becoming "one flesh." Adam and Eve didn't just "have sex"; something much more significant happened. They were united.

The apostle Paul echoes this same idea.

Do you not know that your bodies are members of Christ himself? Shall I then take the members of Christ and unite them with a prostitute? Never! Do you not know that he who united himself with a prostitute is one with her in body? For it is said, "The two will become one flesh." *(1 Corinthians 6:15–16 TNIV)*

Our teenagers need to know that the notion of simply "having sex" is not only unbiblical, it is impossible! When two people come together sexually, they become one flesh. They are united—and not just physically. There is more to it than that.

Sex was designed by God as an expression of intimate oneness in body that matches a couple's commitment to oneness in purpose and direction in life. Our students need to know that they are designed to become one with only one other person.

If we don't tell our students the ramifications of sex outside of marriage, we are failing them. The question we must strive to keep in the forefront of their thinking is: are the temporary pleasures derived from sex worth the long-term complications that it causes? My experience as a counselor and pastor has convinced me that the pain caused by sex before marriage far outweighs the pleasure. The pleasure lasts for a moment. The pain can last a lifetime.

God's Design

God knows all of this. That is why his will for our students is abstinence.

This is the will of God, your sanctification; that is, that you abstain from sexual immorality; that each of you know how to possess his own vessel in sanctification and honor, not in lustful passion, like the Gentiles who do not know God; and that no man transgress and defraud his brother in the matter because the Lord is the avenger in all these things, just as we also told you before and solemnly warned you. For God has not called us for the purpose of impurity, but in sanctification. So, he who rejects this is not rejecting man but the God who gives His Holy Spirit to you. *(1 Thessalonians 4:3-8 NASB)*

To be sanctified means to become like Christ in our characters. That is God's design for your students. He wants them to become like his Son. God's will for students is for them to wait.

Why? Because God is against sex? On the contrary. It is because God loves teenagers and wants the best for them. It is because God wants their sexual experiences to be the best they can possibly be. And he knows more about good sex than anyone does . . . after all, he created it.

God is not against your students. He created them. Sex is not for "mature" people. Sex is not for "ready" people. Sex is not for "in love" people. Sex is for *married* people. It is to be reserved for the unique, multifaceted relationship of marriage.

Relationship 101: For Men Only

Since sex is relational, our guys need to be encouraged to redirect their attentions to developing great relational skills, rather than sexual expertise. Sexual experience now does not translate into sexual fulfillment later on. As we have discovered, the very opposite is true.

The best thing the guys in our student ministries can do now to ensure good relationships with their wives later is to learn how to honor and respect the women God has put in their lives—namely, to love their mothers and sisters! As kinky as it sounds, the best way for our young men to prepare for a great sex life later is to learn how to love Mom now! Why? Because great sex is the by-product of a great relationship. And relational skills aren't magically embedded at the altar. They are learned over time.

During adolescence, young men tend to focus on the physical aspect of their relationships with women. Many of them do just enough of the relational part to "get their way." Consequently, many guys move through their teen years without learning anything about loving and honoring women. Instead, they end up using them. Women become objects to be enjoyed rather than cherished. When this happens, young men end up loving women for the way they make them feel, rather than for who they are.

We need to do everything in our power to help them shift their focus from the physical to the relational side of the equation. If they are willing to reprioritize, they will have a much greater chance of keeping the physical and relational in proper balance. The relationship skills they develop now will serve them for the rest of their lives.

The Deal with Girls

Unlike the young men in our groups, the young women tend to focus on the relational side of things, even when there is only a fragile, temporary relationship in place. Ladies generally look for assurances of commitment once things start heating up physically. As the physical involvement increases, a young woman will want more and more reassurance from her boyfriend that he really cares about her. When a sexual relationship ends, a girl suddenly feels insecure, used, and angry. It is why she may quickly rebound into another unhealthy "relationship."

Why this sudden sense of guilt and loss? Because sex is not just physical, it is relational. And women know that deep in their hearts. As sex outside of marriage increases, a woman's security decreases. A girl begins to feel less and less valuable . . . less and less lovable.

As leaders, we must teach that God created young women to be loved, cherished, and honored. We have to brand on their hearts the need to reserve the intimacy of sex for the men who commit to love, cherish, and honor them for a lifetime.

The Culture of Lies

Having removed intimacy from the equation, our culture is left with only the physical aspects of sex to talk about. And talk about them they do! Everywhere our students turn, they are bombarded with misinformation, half-truths, and flat-out lies. Everything is tilted toward the physical.

This endless proliferation of sexually oriented media marketed specifically to teenagers makes our jobs much more difficult. It is not enough for us to redefine the nature of sex for our students. We must also address the one-sided messages they are continually exposed to. Here are six themes that are overtly and covertly woven into the programming and literature aimed at our kids.

1. Everybody is having sex. To begin with, that is not a true statement. Second, it is not an argument for or against anything. It is simply a statement. Our students need to be reminded that those who are not having sex don't talk about it. There's nothing for them to talk about. There is a silent majority among our students. We need to do everything we can to identify and honor that group.

2. You can't live without sex. Nobody says this directly, but it is certainly implied in much of the music of our culture. I have talked to several young women who admitted that they thought boys "had to have sex." They weren't sure where they heard this, but they assumed it was true. One young woman said that she assumed her boyfriend was having sex with somebody, somewhere since she wouldn't sleep with him. It may come as a shock, but no one has ever died from not having sex. Yet thousands of people have died from AIDS and other sexually transmitted diseases (STDs) because of their sexual activities.

3. Sex is a natural part of a loving relationship. So why can't the students that are sexually active maintain long-term, loving relationships? It has been my experience after counseling hundreds of teenagers that sex is one of the primary reasons relationships fall apart. Instead of sex making the relationship better, it drives a wedge between the two parties. If a student wants to know about real, long-term, fulfilling, loving relationships, have them find someone who has one and ask about the essential ingredients of that relationship.

4. Sex is a natural part of growing up. The truth is, sex keeps people from growing up. Our culture argues that the more sexual experiences you have, the more grown-up you become. On the contrary, nature is telling us that it is not natural to have multiple sex partners. There are over fifty types of venereal diseases identified to date. Many are treatable, but incurable. Nature has made it clear: having multiple sexual experiences with multiple partners is not natural.

5. Sex outside of marriage would cease to be a problem if teens would just wear condoms. This widely held myth is the clearest indication that our society has divorced sex from intimacy and relationship. Everybody is warning students about the physical consequences of unprotected sex. Nobody is warning them about the emotional and relational consequences.

The message our students receive is that the only problems related to sex before marriage are disease and pregnancy. If we stamp out unwanted pregnancies and STDs, we will have stamped out all the consequences of premarital sex. Right? Wrong! A condom can't:

✓ Erase a memory

✓ Remove guilt

✓ Restore a student's reputation

✓ Repair a student's self-esteem

6. Sex makes life better. The truth is that sex outside of marriage doesn't make life better; it makes life more complicated. I will never forget a conversation I had with a woman years ago. She was in her early thirties and had been divorced for about eight years. Jenny had only been a Christian about six months when she came to see me. As soon as she sat down, she said, "I have two questions. The first one is about the church, and the second one is personal."

I don't remember her first question. But her second one is forever etched in my memory. She looked me right in the eye and said, "Okay, about sex. Does the stuff in the Bible about sex being only for married people apply to somebody like me or is that just for teenagers?"

At first, I didn't know what to say. I knew what I believed, but I wasn't sure how to communicate it. Jenny noticed my hesitation. She went on to explain that since she had been married before, she wasn't sure if she was expected to remain celibate. From her vantage point, that seemed like an unreasonable expectation.

I had stalled as long as I could. She deserved an answer. But I knew her faith was new and still quite immature. I was just about to launch into my "sex is for marriage" discourse when suddenly a question popped into my mind. To this day, I believe God rescued both of us by turning my thoughts and words in a different direction.

I looked at Jenny and said, "Before I answer that question, let me ask you a question. Has sex outside of your marriage made your life better or more complicated?"

She stared at the floor for a moment, dropped her head, and began to cry. Through the sobs, she was able to force the words, "more complicated." I waited for a minute before I said, "Jenny, that's why God has reserved sex for marriage."

Every day of our students' lives, they are told that sex can have physical consequences. What this generation of students never hears is that there are emotional, mental, and relational consequences as well. No one escapes. These consequences will follow them into one relationship after another and will ultimately affect their marriages. It is up to us to tell them the rest of the story.

I tell our students all the time, "Fire in the fireplace is a wonderful thing. Fire on the carpet has the potential to burn down your house. Sex is like fire. In the right context, it is an awesome thing. But once it is outside the context it was designed for, sex can burn your life and relationships to the ground."

The Envelope Please

If sex is out of the question, then what can they do? How far can they go? If not all the way, how much of the way? How far is too far?

The Bible does not give us a specific answer to that question. But it does give a general principle to follow when helping students make their decisions. In his letter to the Ephesians, the apostle Paul wrote: *"Be very careful, then, how you live—not as unwise but as wise" (5:15).* The question our students must learn to ask is, "What is the wise thing for me to do?" The writer of Proverbs tells us that *"He who trusts in himself is a fool, but he who walks in wisdom is kept safe" (28:26).* Choosing the way of wisdom in the realm of purity will lead to safety.

Common sense is one facet of wisdom. Here are four common-sense principles to teach your students as they wrestle with the question: How far is too far?

1. The further you go, the faster you go. On the
continuum that moves a couple from, "Hi, my name is . . ." to

intercourse, there are many transition points. Students need to understand that every time their physical involvement moves to a new level, their sense of fulfillment passes quicker than it did at the previous level. The further they move toward intercourse, the more rapidly their desire accelerates.

2. The further you go, the further you want to go.

We can all remember the sensation we had the first time we held hands with that "special someone." At that moment, holding hands was enough. It was almost too much! But before long, the thrill began to wear off. So we took the physical relationship to the next level.

Teenagers need to understand that their sexual appetites are somewhat like their appetites for food. They are never fully and finally satisfied. When you feed an appetite, you increase both the capacity and intensity of it. If you have ever tried to eat half of a dessert, you know what I mean. It is easier not to eat any. The more you eat, the more you want to eat.

Our students need to know that drawing a line mentally does nothing to stem their desires physically. They will always want to go further. I stress this point because kids have a tendency to reason this way: *well, if we could just take it one step further, that would be enough.* But the truth is, short of intercourse, there is no "ultimate" satisfaction. Our bodies were designed to go "all the way."

Again, appetites are never fully and finally satisfied.

3. The further you go, the harder it is to go back. Stuart shared this story with me . . .

Layla came to my wife at a camp with tears streaming
down her face and a heart that was heavy with guilt.
Layla told of how she had been forbidden by her father
to see a particular guy. She disobeyed her dad and had
been seeing him behind his back. They had been sexually
involved for several months and she wanted so badly to
stop.

That July, Layla resolved in her heart to end the
relationship with Grant. She was a different girl from
July to December. God began to move in her in ways that
were obvious to all, and Layla became a leader in our
ministry. Grant kept calling, but she resisted his pleas
for a second chance.

Just after Christmas, she decided, out of kindness, to
go and see him. The principle of "the further a student
goes physically, the harder it is to go back" became a
scar she will wear for the rest of her life. Instead of
starting at the beginning, Layla and Grant picked up
where they had left off. Layla got pregnant. My wife
took her to the doctor to confirm what she knew in her
heart. I had the heartbreaking task of telling her mom
and dad.

Our students need to know that God did not design them to go back. He designed them with the desire to move forward sexually. Consequently, it is almost impossible to permanently retreat to safety once certain lines have been crossed.

4. Where you draw the line determines three important things:

✓ The arena of your temptation

If a young man decides that the line for him is kissing, then he has determined what he will be tempted to do next; namely, whatever he perceives the next step to be after kissing. On the other end of the spectrum, if a young man determines that oral sex is okay, then he has determined the arena of his temptation as well. Our students need to know that every conviction has a corresponding temptation. When they settle their standards, they determine their temptations.

✓ The intensity of your temptation

Temptation increases with increased passion. Passion increases as a couple moves closer and closer to intercourse. Every couple is going to be tempted. Where they draw the line determines the intensity of the temptation.

As you guide your students through the exercise of setting standards, ask them, "Assuming you are going to be tempted to go further than you choose, how intense do you want that temptation to be?" Remind them that where they draw the line determines the intensity of their temptation. They are actually choosing the level of pressure they will feel in their dating relationships.

✓ The consequences of giving in to temptation

Where a student draws the line determines the consequence of giving in to temptation. If a couple has decided that holding hands is far enough and they get carried away and actually kiss, what are the consequences? A touch of guilt, perhaps. Worst case scenario: somebody gets strep throat. But if a couple has drawn the line at the edge of intercourse . . . you get the picture.

Our students need to know that they are, in a sense, determining their own destinies by where they draw the line. From time to time, passions run high and kids will temporarily abandon their standards. Where they have drawn the line will determine the nature of the consequences once that line is crossed.

A Pointed Question

The whole "How far is too far?" issue is so confusing for our kids. It doesn't help that they are immersed in a culture that thinks the question is bogus to begin with. The issue for most of their friends is "How far *can* I go?" not "How far *should* I go?"

When I was moving through the maze of adolescence, a different question brought this whole issue into focus for me: how far will I want the woman I spend the rest of my life with to have gone with the person she dated right before meeting me? I really hated that question. It may have been difficult for me to determine how far I should go, but I knew exactly how far the person I would one day marry should go—not very far.

Unfortunately, many of our students are already living with the regret of having gotten too involved sexually. Obviously, those students need to be reassured of God's grace and forgiveness. But they need to be challenged along with the rest of your kids.

Whenever I talk to students about sex, I always remind them that regardless of what has happened in the past, they can begin again. The fact that they have gone "too far" is no reason to give up the fight and give in to temptation. I remind them that someday they will meet someone they would like to spend the rest of their lives with. When they do, they will have one of three stories to tell.

Story One

When I was a teenager, I messed up. My boyfriend (girlfriend) and I got carried away sexually. I reasoned that since I did it once, it really didn't matter if I did it again. So I slept with several other people along the way.

Story Two

When I was a teenager, I messed up sexually. But when I was __ years old, after hearing my student pastor teach on moral boundaries, I decided that God knew what he was talking about. Sex was created for marriage. So I decided to wait. I set new standards and have stuck with them. Since that day, I have saved myself for you.

Story Three

When I was a teenager, I realized that God knew more about sex than anyone. Since he created sex for marriage, I decided to wait. So I have saved myself for you.

Then I ask two questions: "Which story do you want to tell?" and "Which story do you want to hear from the person you choose to marry?" I tell them to make their decisions accordingly.

Conclusion

If one of your students were waiting at a bus stop, he wouldn't necessarily get on the first bus that pulled up to the stop. He would look to see where it was going. Every day, students are being invited to get on board a bus that is taking thousands of their peers to lives of misery and pain. Before our students board that bus, they need to check out the destination. It is up to us to sensitize them to both the truth about sex and the lies our culture continues to manufacture.

Purity paves the way to intimacy. And in the end, intimacy is what will provide our teenagers with the context for satisfying sexual experiences.

Checking In
Checkpoint: Moral Boundaries

Bible Study Assignment:

✓ Read 1 Corinthians 6:18.

✓ Read 1 Thessalonians 4:3–8 in the NASB.

Questions:

✓ Revisit the six themes and write down specific television shows, movies, and songs that promote these themes to students.

_____

_____

_____

✓ In 1 Corinthians 6:18, how does Paul encourage us to deal with immorality? _____

_____

_____

✓ How would you define immorality? Why do you think immorality is a sin against your own body? _____

_____

_____

_____

✓ What does Paul mean by "your sanctification" in 1 Thessalonians 4:3–8? _____

_____

_____

_____

✓ What three things does Paul say are God's will for you in relation to this sanctification? _____

_____

_____

_____

✓ What does Paul mean by "defrauding" a brother as it relates to sexuality? _____

_____

_____

_____

✓ What do you think Paul means when he says, "the Lord is the avenger in all these things"? _____

_____

_____

_____

Checkpoint #4

Meaningful Friendships

DETERMINING THE QUALITY AND DIRECTION OF OUR LIVES

If you sleep with dogs, you are going to get fleas.

—Southern proverb

Concept

Meaningful Friendships

Principle

Our friends determine the direction and quality of our lives.

Critical Question

Are your students establishing healthy friendships and avoiding unhealthy ones?

Key Passage

Proverbs 13:20

Meaningful Friendships
DILEMMA

All of us would agree that our friends have a significant impact on our lives. Perhaps you came to faith in Christ because of a friend. I'm sure you can recount memories of when you and your friends got into trouble or did something you now regret. Our friends have played major roles in determining the direction and quality of our lives.

As it relates to students, recent research has shown that the greatest influence in a teenager's life is another teenager. In the 1960s, a Gallup poll showed that the top three influences in a teenager's life were:

1. Parents

2. Teachers

3. Spiritual leaders

But the playing field has shifted dramatically. According to a more recent survey, the top three influences in a teenager's life are:

1. Friends

2. Media (music, television, movies, etc.)

3. Parents

(Not to discourage you, but spiritual leaders had dropped to number seventeen on the list. Essentially, we do not exist!)

Our response to this stunning shift in influence should be obvious. As leaders, we must ensure that students understand the influence their friends have in their lives. As parents, we must not let our teenagers' friends "out accept" us. We must do everything we can to ensure that the peers that influence our students are leading them in God's direction. Our students' friends are going to affect them in significant ways.

But just how big of an impact do they make?

As we will see, Scripture teaches that friends are one of the most powerful influences in your students' lives.

The Three Amigos

A great illustration of this principle is a story Stuart tells:

I will never forget a couple of my friends from third grade. Bradley, Gary, and I were like "the three amigos." We were always getting into trouble, always causing chaos, and always inventing some new way of becoming infamous.

One day Bradley and Gary decided we should seal our bond. They made me take the "sissy test." A person would take the eraser end of a pencil and rub it on the back of your hand as fast as he could until your hand bled or you screamed. If you screamed, you were a "sissy" and no longer a friend. I screamed *and* bled. And I screamed again when I got home and my dad found out what I had done.

Think about this. I became a "sissy," gained a scar, lost my friends, and got a spanking—all because of the powerful influence of my friends. Before you laugh too hard, think back. Chances are you did some ridiculous things at the urging of friends as well.

The question we must ask ourselves is this: are our students establishing healthy friendships and avoiding unhealthy ones? The answer to that question will play a major role in how they conduct themselves throughout middle school and high school. The answer to that question will determine where our students end up in their journeys. Why? Because the friends they choose will determine the direction and quality of their lives.

The Evidence

Some might be tempted to argue with the previous statement. So here are a few observations that substantiate this rather extreme claim.

1. Friends often have greater influence over a teenager than a teenager's own *convictions.*

Eventually, our students will have to choose between their friends and their convictions. When I ask teenagers to raise their hands if they have ever temporarily abandoned a conviction at the urging of a friend, every hand in the room goes up. Most of our students don't have to reach back too far to remember an occasion when they were forced to choose between the acceptance of their friends and their deeply held convictions.

This dynamic explains why so many camp decisions are abandoned within hours of the church bus pulling back into the parking lot. Taylor makes a decision for Christ at a camp or a retreat. He leaves the commitment service determined to do the right thing, to make some real changes. The partying is going to stop. He is going to break it off with his girlfriend. No more lying to his parents. And what happens? Taylor goes back to an environment where the need for acceptance outweighs his convictions. Gradually, he slips back into the life that he renounced at camp. Why? Because Taylor's friends have a greater influence on him than his convictions.

2. Friends often have a greater influence on a teenager than the teenager's *parents.*

This is baffling. It is especially baffling when we consider the sacrifices the average parent makes for his or her child. One would think that out of sheer gratitude students would continue to give Mom and Dad the lion's share of their devotion. But that wasn't the case when *we* were teenagers. And it is certainly not the case now.

On paper, it doesn't make any sense that a fourteen-year-old would put more stock in the advice of another fourteen-year-old than he would in the advice of the man and woman who would die for him at a moment's notice. But he does. That's the power of friendship.

With the tragic breakdown of today's family structure, our students' friends have even greater leverage in their lives. If students don't feel unconditional acceptance at home, they will find it with their friends. This explains in part the sudden rise in the formation of gangs. What was once considered an inner-city problem now haunts tiny towns in Middle America. For many teenagers, both male and female, the gang has replaced the family unit as the primary environment of acceptance. In most cases, a teenager's peers have taken the reins of influence away from Mom and Dad.

3. Our teenagers' friends often have greater influence over them than *God*.

Ask your students if friends have ever influenced them to do things they knew were contrary to God's will for their lives. Sure they have. We all have!

In other words, some sixteen-year-old one of your daughters has known for all of four months is able to persuade her to temporarily turn her back on the God of the universe in order to do something she won't even remember in a year and that could potentially change the trajectory of her life for years to come. That is a lot of power. Think about it—a sixteen-year-old that has the power to out-influence God.

Now you can see why we say that your students' friends will determine the direction and quality of their lives. Nobody can compete. Not even God.

The Proof

This principle is supported by more than mere observation. Solomon, the wisest person who ever lived, said, *"He who walks with the wise grows wise, but a companion of fools suffers harm"* (Proverbs 13:20).

Both a promise and a warning are included in this verse. The promise is that if your students walk with wise friends, then they, in turn, will grow wise. The warning is that students who associate themselves with fools will suffer harm. Let's take a closer look at each side of this equation.

The Promise

If students spend the majority of their time with wise people, they will become wise. In other words, the "wise" will rub off on them. But what does that mean? What does it mean to be wise? And is it really that important? If our students don't understand the benefits of being wise, this verse doesn't provide much leverage. But if somehow we are able to create a thirst in their hearts for wisdom, then this verse has the potential to redirect their thinking about friends.

One of the most productive series I did for our students was built around the three types of people mentioned in the book of Proverbs: the wise, the fool, and the scoffer. I used a concordance to look up every verse in Proverbs that mentioned these characters. Then I made a list of the terms and phrases that describe each. I spent several weeks talking to our students about the benefits and blessings associated with wisdom. For many of the teenagers in our group, that study did more to create a hunger for wisdom than anything else we did. Once that transformation began to take place, the significance of Proverbs 13:20 began to take hold in their lives.

The pursuit of wisdom will do more over the long run to motivate your students to rethink their friendships than anything else you can do. Create a hunger in their hearts for wisdom, and you will have the tool you need to redirect their relationships.

Hard to Spot

A wise person is the one who knows the difference between right and wrong and chooses to do what's right—even when it's hard. Whereas unwise teenagers are easy to spot, the wise are harder to find. In fact, your students may be quick to object to this whole principle by arguing that they don't know any "wise" students. If wisdom is the primary criteria for friendship, they may feel as if they are facing the prospect of having no friends at all.

Wise people are somewhat like owls. They are out there, but they are hard to spot. Why? For one thing, owls are quiet. They are still. They tend to blend in with the environment without causing a scene. The few times I have seen owls in their natural habitats were when someone pointed them out to me. When they do make noise, it is significant. More times than not, however, finding those wise people becomes a process of elimination.

That's the way it is in finding wise friends. Students need to understand that wise students *are* difficult to find. By observing (from a safe distance) the consequences suffered by the students who make poor choices, your students will be better able to choose healthy friendships.

Several years ago, there was a beer commercial on television with the tag line "Good times are made for good friends . . . it doesn't get any better than this." The scene that would slowly emerge was a group of friends sitting around a lakeside campfire, drinking beer and eating fresh fish cooked over an open fire. The obvious implication was that beer created good times that could only be experienced with good friends.

Our students need to be reminded that good friends are wise friends. Good friends know the difference between right and wrong. Good friends make good decisions. And it will always be easier for them to do the right thing when they are with the right people.

The Warning

Proverbs 13:20 contains a warning as well—a warning that most of your students will quickly identify with: *"A companion of fools suffers harm."*

In other words, if your students spend the majority of their time with fools, they will suffer painful consequences.

A fool is someone who knows the difference between right and wrong but chooses to do what is wrong. Fools just don't care about doing what's right. They are not ignorant; they just aren't interested. Pointing out the consequences of an action does not stop a fool; he just does what he wants to do when he wants to do it. A fool feels that he is invincible.

Notice what the writer of Proverbs says about the *"companion of fools."* Hanging around a fool doesn't mean you become a fool. It's worse than that: something bad will eventually happen to you. Associating with foolish friends doesn't necessarily mean your students will become fools themselves. What it does mean, according to Proverbs, is that your students are unintentionally putting themselves in harm's way. They have made themselves targets. It doesn't say harm *might* happen. It clearly states that the friends of fools *will suffer harm*.

One of the recurring arguments that every parent and student pastor is forced to address goes something like this: "But I don't do what they do. I just want to be where they are." Specifically, "I don't drink. I just go to the parties."

Our students need to understand the principle behind this potent warning. Oftentimes, it is not what we do that causes us to suffer harm. It is who we are with. It is the companion of fools . . . not necessarily the fools . . . that will suffer harm.

A Painful Reminder

Stuart shared this story . . .

For all of us who knew Josh Ming, Saturday, April 9, 1994, will always serve as a cruel reminder of this principle. Josh was driving his cousin and two female passengers to a house in Shreveport, Louisiana, when four teenagers, standing in the street, began firing on their car. Josh was shot in the back of the head and killed in what police described as a "hail of gunfire." Fifty-plus bullets hit their car.

The four teenagers arrested in connection with the fatal shooting were known members of a gang of middle- and upper-class teens called The Fighting Irish. Josh's cousin was suspected of being involved in gang activity, as were the two girls in the car.

Josh was just giving his cousin a ride.

But Josh was not a fool. He had given his life to Christ, and the change had been evident. Josh participated regularly at our weekly outreach events. He helped teach our children's choir with his girlfriend, Jennifer. He was a member of the Airline High School football team. His grades were improving. Life was good. On this one night, however, he was the companion of fools, and he suffered harm.

Again, the focus of this warning is not on *what* a student does. The focus is on *who* your students are with.

Under the Influence

I think most students recognize that their friends have an impact on their lives. But few of them understand why they are so susceptible to their influence. It is difficult for any of us to break a pattern of behavior if we don't know what's driving us in that direction. Students need to understand the often-unidentified dynamic that drives their friendships. Most of them operate under the assumption that they have freely chosen their friends. But nothing could be further from the truth.

Gravitational Pull

If some teenagers in your ministry approached you and asked how they should choose their friends, what would you say? Would you tell them to interview candidates? Would you advise them to walk around looking for those who had all the characteristics you desire for their friends to have? Think about it. What does it mean when we talk about "choosing friends"?

Your students don't really choose their friends. If they did, we probably wouldn't need to include this checkpoint. If they were carefully "choosing" friends, their networks of relationships would look much different. From time to time, I would ask my students to make a list of the top five qualities they want in a friend. Then I would ask them to list five qualities they want in the people they date.

Over and over students would admit that their current friendships and dating relationships fell short of what they really hoped for. Why? Because they didn't choose those friends. If they had "chosen" their friends, they would have held out until those who made the cut came along.

Again, teenagers don't choose their friends. Instead, they gravitate toward acceptance; they hook up with the kids who are most accepting of them. Like all of us, they are acceptance magnets. They gravitate toward environments of acceptance.

Watch students walk into a party and you will witness this principle in action. Those students will naturally begin to communicate and interact with other students who make them feel accepted. They will avoid the students or groups of students they sense will reject them.

The same holds true for students who change schools. One of our students recently changed schools to get away from a group of friends that was not a good influence on him. It has been interesting to watch the people this student gravitates toward. Sometimes changing schools is not the answer, because students are naturally going to interact with those peers who accept them . . . *their friends choose them.*

You've seen it. Teenagers in your group make decisions about their appearance and conduct based primarily on how it will affect their standing with the students to whom they are looking for acceptance. Teenagers try to wring acceptance out of just about every environment they work, play, and live in.

This is why some of your students can act so spiritual at church and live like the devil on the weekends. They want to fit in and are willing to adapt to the environments that offer the acceptance they need. After all, everybody wants to be liked by somebody.

Bottom line—their desire to be accepted has more to do with who they build relationships with than a list of characteristics they are looking for in a friend. They don't "choose" their friends. Again, they gravitate toward environments of acceptance.

So Prove It

When I challenge students with this concept, they are usually quick to take offense. On the surface, it sounds like I am making them all out to be extremely insecure. So I ask them the following three questions:

1. Have you ever lied to keep from looking bad?

Sure they have. Why? Because they would rather lie than face the rejection of "friends." As a follow-up question I ask, "How many of you believe it is wrong to lie?" They all raise their hands.

My point is that they have been willing to abandon a conviction for the sake of acceptance. They have been willing to lie to avoid rejection.

2. Have you ever stolen something you didn't need because somebody you were with stole something?

Sheepishly, a few hands go up. Mostly guys. Then I ask, "How many of you believe stealing is wrong?" All the hands go up. Again, I have illustrated the incredible power of acceptance and the innate fear of rejection. To take one last dig, I will ask, "If you were making a list of things you want in a friend, how many of you would include 'thief'?" No hands.

I know a girl who was suspended from high school for several days during her sophomore year for shoplifting alcohol from a grocery store. Get this: she did it while she was on a school field trip (not the sharpest tool in the shed). Later she admitted she didn't even drink. She was doing it for her "friends."

3. How many of you have friends who have self-destructive habits you have never said anything about?

Then I ask, "Why?" If you are really their friend, why don't you confront them? Eventually they'll admit they don't want to make them mad or appear to be nosey. In other words, they are not willing to risk losing the friendship even if it means possibly saving the life of a friend.

The point of all this is to help students understand that they have surrounded themselves with people whose acceptance is more important than their own convictions, their own integrity, and even the welfare of the people they consider to be friends.

They didn't choose these people as friends. They simply found an environment of acceptance.

The Influence Principle

Acceptance is a good thing. There is nothing wrong with wanting to be accepted. But acceptance by the wrong people can be detrimental. Why? Because acceptance paves the way to influence.

> **Acceptance by a friend is more important than the friend.**

This is a principle that student pastors, youth workers, and parents need to keep in front of them at all times. Acceptance and influence are inexorably linked. Within a relationship, you can't have sustained influence apart from acceptance. Students resist the influence of those they don't feel accepted by but drop their guards when they feel accepted.

What this means is that our student environments and homes must be the most accepting places our students experience. We must "out accept" the competition. That is the only way we will develop sustained influence with our students. They won't embrace our message until they are assured of our love and acceptance.

The Other Side

As we mentioned earlier in this checkpoint, acceptance is only one side of the coin. Our students not only gravitate toward acceptance, they flee environments of rejection. Nothing hurts like rejection. They will go to extreme measures to avoid it.

Stuart recounted this story from his childhood.

Because of our financial status growing up, I never had the coolest, brand-name clothes in school. One year, my parents bought me two pairs of Sears Tuffskins jeans for school: a brown pair and a blue pair. All the cool kids had Levi's with the silver or red tabs . . . I had two pairs of Tuffskins that had to last all year. When my jeans started wearing out and getting holes in them, my mom, who was big into cross-stitching, made a huge Indian head on the leg of my brown jeans and an American flag on the rear end of my blue jeans. I can still hear kids pledging allegiance to my rear end and calling me "Tonto." I vowed that I would never have to face that kind of rejection again.

Most teenagers have been laughed at or put down enough to know they want to avoid rejection at any cost. Eric Harris, one of the two young gunmen in the Columbine High School tragedy, wrote in his academic day planner, "The lonely man strikes with absolute rage." Harris and Dylan Klebold both wrote of not fitting in, of not being accepted. Investigators who analyzed the writings said, "They plotted against all those persons who found them offensive—jocks, girls that said no, other outcasts, or anybody they thought did not accept them" (Steven K. Paulson, "Columbine Journals Showed Anger").

The Big But

If you were to ask students to define a good friend, they would probably list all kinds of qualities: good listener, loyal, honest, someone I like to be with. But for many students, friendship is defined by acceptance alone.

This explains why some kids in your group can't seem to break away from destructive relationships. To leave the relationships means abandoning an environment of acceptance. That is hard to do . . . especially when there doesn't seem to be another safe harbor. Simply pointing out to students the consequences of the relationships is not enough to get them to make changes. Acceptance covers a multitude of consequences.

In light of the overwhelming power of acceptance, we as student leaders must help students choose what they want out of life before they allow someone to choose them as friends. Setting a course for their lives will help students eliminate friends that will not help them reach their goals and potential. Otherwise, it is like shooting a hole in the side of a wall and then painting a target and bull's-eye around that hole. In other words, our students will determine the direction of their lives by who they run with rather than what they could become and accomplish. Peers replace potential.

I have never seen students make major, long-lasting changes in their lives without making some changes in the area of friendships. Like you, I have seen students make all sorts of commitments. But until students are willing to tackle this sticky area, progress is generally short-lived. It is almost impossible for students to change their focus and direction in life without adjusting who they surround themselves with.

For Those Who Choose to Choose

Acceptance *is* an important part of a friendship. But it is only one part. After all, students who end up in drug-rehabilitation units or detention centers have a group of friends that accepts them. Oftentimes, those friends got them involved in the very things that messed them up to begin with. Acceptance is important. But it isn't enough.

God wants our students to have real friends, not just people who accept them. So, what should our students be looking for in the people they allow into their inner circles? What do *real* friends look like?

True Friends

True friends will *love* them and not just *accept* them. You can accept people without truly loving them. But if you truly love someone, you will certainly accept him. True friends are ones who accept your students just as they are—but who love them too much to leave them that way.

In a friendship where acceptance is the only thing that holds the relationship together, there will be little confrontation. Nobody will be willing to risk it. Nobody will say the things that need to be said.

But true friends are more committed to their friends than to their friendships—more concerned about what's best for their friends than they are about being accepted. Chris Farley is a tragic example of this. How many times have we heard people who considered themselves Chris's best friends bemoan his tragic death? Yet they admit they would never confront him on his alcohol and drug abuse. They chose to ignore these obvious issues for the sake of Chris's acceptance. After all, he was famous. They were so enamored with what they gained from the relationship that they ignored what was best for their "friend." Apparently, they were more committed to the friendship than the friend.

The BIG Relationship

In a friendship that is built on love and acceptance, there will be healthy respect for each other's convictions. For our students who are Christians, this translates into friends who respect and encourage their relationship with God.

When I was a student pastor, I constantly quizzed the students in our youth group about this. I was always asking, "Do your friends encourage or hinder your walk with Christ?" A true friend, Christian or not, will encourage the deeply held convictions of another. Our students need to guard against friendships that slowly chip away at their convictions.

We need to remind them often that they are never to sacrifice their relationship with God for a relationship with another person. They must decide which relationship is going to take priority.

Counterfeit Friends

People who accept our teenagers but don't have their best interests in mind are counterfeit friends. Just as there is counterfeit money, there are counterfeit friends. Students need to know how to spot one. For the most part, a counterfeit friend looks like a friend, acts like a friend, feels like a friend, and is usually attempting to be a friend. But he or she isn't the genuine item.

A counterfeit friend is far worse than an enemy. Our students' enemies can hurt them temporarily, but counterfeit friends can ruin their lives. With enemies, our guards are up. But when we are with friends, we are wide open to their influence.

This is why our greatest regrets usually involve people we thought were our friends.

Specifically, two things make counterfeit friends dangerous:

1. A counterfeit reduces our incentive for seeking out the real thing.

If you had an endless supply of counterfeit money that was accepted everywhere as the real thing, how motivated would you be to work? Why labor for the real thing when the counterfeit works just as well?

If a counterfeit friend provides acceptance, why work at developing new and genuine relationships? Students who have surrounded themselves with counterfeit friends don't feel a need to add anybody else to their inner circles. We may see their need for more wholesome relationships, but they don't. Many times, it is not until the counterfeit is removed that teenagers find the incentive to begin looking for the real thing.

2. A counterfeit is hard to leave behind.

Think about how difficult it would be to toss a bagful of counterfeit hundred dollar bills into a fire. It is difficult to leave a counterfeit behind. It is difficult for our students to end relationships with counterfeit friends.

I tell our students all the time, "The most difficult thing you will do as a teenager is walk away from relationships with people you really care about." It is difficult, but it is necessary.

Spotting a Counterfeit

Our students need to consider three things as they evaluate the genuineness of their friendships.

1. Direction of the Relationship

Relationships don't stand still. They are always moving in one direction or another. Students have a tendency to evaluate a friendship based on where it is at a point in time. They need to become sensitive to the *direction* of a relationship as well as what is happening at any given moment.

Genuine friendships move in a positive, mutually beneficial direction. A counterfeit friend will move the relationship the other way. Our students need to ask, "If this relationship continues to move in the current direction, where will it end up?" And then, "Is that where I want to be?"

2. Self-destructive Behavior

Counterfeit friends will usually exhibit some form of self-destructive behavior. We call them "toxic" friends. The reason this is important to look out for is that if their friends won't take care of themselves, they certainly won't be looking out for the best interests of our teenagers. If somebody doesn't take good care of his car, I will certainly think twice before I loan him mine.

3. Lack of Solid Conviction

Any "friend" who lacks convictions will have a difficult time being a true friend. We need to teach our students to be listening for statements such as:

"You have to do what you feel is right."

"Everybody has to decide for himself."

"Nobody can tell another person what is right for him or her."

Such are the mantras of those who drift with the emotion of the moment.

So Then, What?

So, what are kids to do once they realize that those they thought were their friends are counterfeits? One of the best ways to address this important question is to introduce them to the concentric circles of friendship.

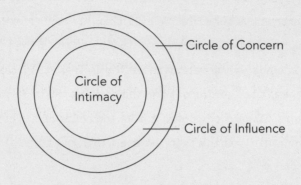

The concentric circles diagram will allow your students to keep this sensitive subject in proper perspective. If we are not careful, students will get the idea that we don't care about their friends. Or, that we don't want them to have relationships with peers that need Christ. The concentric-circles-of-concern diagram allows students to see that the issue is not whether or not their friends are "good people," as much as it is the health and direction of the relationships.

Explain that all of their friends fall into one of three categories. The outer circle represents the friends they are concerned about. These may be their non-Christian friends. It may be Christian friends who are going through tough times. It is anybody they are concerned about. These are peers your students hope to influence.

The second circle, the circle of influence, represents the

friends your students allow to influence them. Our teenagers know who the positive and negative influences are in their lives.

The third circle, the circle of intimacy, is reserved for one person. It is reserved for the man or woman a student will meet someday, fall in love with, and marry. Including this category will remind your students of the importance of whom they date. They need to choose the people they date from their circles of influence, not their circles of concern. It is easy for kids to allow their feelings of mercy and concern to evolve into romantic interests.

Once they understand the relationship of the circles, the issue then becomes what to do with the friends in the circle of influence who are negative influences.

As you might guess, students must move counterfeit friends out of their circles of influence and into their circles of concern. What that actually means will depend upon the circumstances surrounding the friendships. But the bottom line is that there must be some changes.

This is a painful process. We've all seen our kids struggle with this. As I said earlier, the most difficult thing our teenagers will be called upon to do is walk away from relationships with people they really care about. It is difficult, but it is necessary. After all, their friends, especially those within their circles of influence, *will determine the direction and quality of their lives.*

What Are the Options?

When it comes to moving counterfeit friends out of their circles of influence, your students have three options. They can do nothing. This usually means choosing not to decide. But time is their enemy, not their ally, when it comes to counterfeit friends.

A second option is for them to take a step back. By that, I mean that your students can adjust the amount of time they spend with particular friends. In addition, they can take steps to take more control of the relationships. They can begin conducting the friendships on their terms, rather than on those of their friends. For example:

✓ They can host the relationship rather than spending time at their friend's house.

✓ They can begin choosing the movies, music, videos, etc.

✓ They can drive instead of riding.

✓ They can choose the places to hang out.

In this option, your students lead the relationships; they set the pace. If their friends won't go along, then they may have to move toward the third option.

The final measure in moving friends out of the circle of influence is stepping away from the relationship altogether. Students will most likely object by saying, "What's going to happen to them if I just walk away?" The real issue is what is going to happen to your students if they *don't*.

Again, friends determine the direction and quality of our lives. We know that from personal experience. Let's do all we can to ingrain this simple principle into the minds and hearts of our students.

Checking In

Checkpoint: Meaningful Friendships

Bible Study Assignment:

✓ Read Proverbs 13:20.

✓ Read Proverbs 14:8.

✓ Read Proverbs 13:10.

Questions:

✓ According to Proverbs 13:20, what is the result of having a relationship with a wise person? _____

_____

_____

_____

✓ What is the result of having a relationship with a fool?_____

_____

_____

_____

✓ Who wrote Proverbs? Do you think the writer gave validity to this principle? _____

_____

_____

_____

✓ Read Proverbs 14:8. What is the wisdom of the prudent?____

_____

_____

_____

✓ What is the folly of the fool?_____

_____

_____

_____

✓ What do these two extremes mean to you?_____

_____

_____

_____

✓ Read Proverbs 13:10. According to this verse, what is the root cause of the chaos that follows a fool? _____

_____

_____

_____

Checkpoint #5

Wise Choices

WALKING WISELY IN A FOOL'S WORLD

May God grant us the wisdom to discover the right,
the will to choose it, and the strength to make it endure.

—King Arthur in *First Knight*

Concept

Wise Choices

Critical Question

Are your students making wise choices?

Principle

Walk wisely

Key Passage

Ephesians 5:15–17

WISE CHOICES
DILEMMA

Whenever students are faced with opportunities, invitations, or desires, they will eventually pose the question "Is there anything wrong with this?" The assumption is that if something is not wrong, then it must be right. If they have never heard a sermon against it, if there aren't any verses about it, or if other Christians are involved, most teenagers instinctively reach the conclusion that it must be all right. Gradually, without even realizing it, they are really asking this question: *how close can I get to sin without actually sinning?*

The "How far is too far?" issue we discussed in checkpoint #3 is a great example of this. Students want to know how far they can go in a physical relationship with a boyfriend or girlfriend before they are sinning. Where is that line? Many of our students want to avoid sin. At the same time, they don't want to miss any legitimate fun.

Teenagers have a propensity to live on the line. If life were a winding mountain road, they'd take it on two wheels at ninety miles an hour instead of slowing down and staying a safe distance from the edge. Why do they live like that? Their behavior stems from their insatiable curiosity—shared by many adults—to find out how close they can get to sin without actually sinning.

So, how close *can* they get? The Bible doesn't answer that question directly. As student ministers, we've tried to meander our way through a complex myriad of biblical principles and form some type of foundational answer for this question and others like it. But students eventually see through our uncertainty. And if we aren't careful, they will exit our student ministries with no answers to some very important questions.

✓ Can I date non-Christians?

✓ What type of music can I listen to?

✓ How far is too far?

✓ Can I attend parties?

✓ Is it all right for me to have a beer?

✓ Which movies can I watch?

Beyond Life on the Line

This unresolved tension leads many of our students to live dangerously close to sin. Consequently, they fall to the same temptations over and over until they are tempted to believe that the Christian life just doesn't work.

The solution to this dilemma is *not* recommitment or rededication. As long as students are living on that line, increasing their commitment level doesn't do any good. Recommitment while living on the edge of "too far" is like an alcoholic standing at a bar and swearing he will never drink again.

Instead of evaluating opportunities, relationships, and invitations by the standard of "Is anything wrong with this?" students need to ask a new question—a question that takes them to the heart of the issues they struggle with daily. When faced with an opportunity, invitation, or desire, the most appropriate question a student can ask is, "Is this the *wise* thing to do?"

In order to drive this principle home, I developed a statement that summarizes this principle in a slightly creative fashion.

> There's good and there's bad . . .
> But that is not our cue.
> But rather . . .
> What is the wise thing to do?

Easy Does It

The apostle Paul encouraged the believers in Ephesus to examine all of life through the lens of wisdom. He instructed them: *"Be careful how you walk, not as unwise men but as wise, making the most of your time, because the days are evil. So then do not be foolish, but understand what the will of the Lord is"* (5:15–17 NASB).

As believers, we are to walk wisely. God wants us to learn

how to anticipate trouble, not walk blindly into it. The term "careful" carries with it the idea of scoping out a situation. Again, God wants us to anticipate things before it is too late to avoid them.

Whether they realize it or not, our students live in a world that is designed to destroy their minds, their relationships, their self-esteem, and their bodies. The world they live in is a dangerous place. This is what Paul was referring to when he said, "The days are evil." They were evil then, and they are evil now. I cannot imagine being sixteen in this generation. Yet God has given us the charge of loving and protecting the teenagers who are navigating through this culture. Loving and protecting entails teaching them how to live in a dangerous world.

No Foolishness Allowed

Dangerous environments require extraordinary precautions. Think of all the equipment a firefighter puts on before rushing into a burning building. Or think of all the checks, double-checks, and triple-checks NASA goes through before sending a manned shuttle into space. That environment demands meticulous precautions. That's why Paul went on to say, *"Do not be foolish."* In other words, don't lose sight of the nature of what is going on around you. Students cannot approach life blindly, as if all is well.

Most of us know from experience that we are just one

decision away from doing irreversible damage to our lives and relationships. Time and maturity have taught us. Many of us have scars to remind us. But our students are naive. In their naïveté, they are prone to approach their world as if it is a safe place. Part of our responsibility is to paint a realistic picture of what is lurking out there in the "real world." And beyond warning them, we must equip them to avoid those relationships and opportunities that have the potential to hurt them.

Wisdom is one of God's primary navigational tools for life. When students learn to run everything that comes their way through the grid of "Is this the wise thing to do?" they have taken a big step in preparing themselves for these "evil days."

Understand!

The apostle Paul ended his admonition with a fascinating charge. He said, *"Understand what the will of the Lord is"* (v. 17).

This was puzzling to me at first. How can he command us to "understand" something? After all, if you don't understand something, being told to "understand" does nothing to lift you out of your confusion.

Paul is saying, "Face up to what you know in your heart is the will of the Lord." In teaching our students to make wise decisions, we must also help them face what they know in their hearts to be true. As long as they aren't being honest with themselves, wisdom will elude them.

For example, if a certain group of friends continuously gets them in trouble, students need to find the courage and humility to admit it. If certain forms of entertainment cause them to sin, students must be honest with themselves about it. If certain songs send their minds in directions they shouldn't go, it is time they admit that as well. Once our students are willing to face the truth that is rattling around in their hearts, the wise choices will become apparent.

The Un-Plan

Another key passage that deals with the subject of wisdom is Proverbs 28:26. The writer of Proverbs says, *"He who trusts in his own heart is a fool, but he who walks wisely will be delivered"* (NASB).

God promises to protect those who walk wisely. He promises to deliver them. Deliver them from what? Think about it. What would you have been delivered from in your teenage years if you had made wise choices? Guilt? Bad memories? A ruined reputation? Impurity? Scars?

Let's face it. Our students don't stay up late at night planning to get into trouble. Sin and consequences always surprise them. Nothing, it seems, is ever intentional. No doubt you've heard statements like these:

✓ "I don't know how it happened."

✓ "I didn't know he would . . ."

✓ "I didn't know it was spiked."

✓ "I didn't plan to . . ."

✓ "It was the first time."

The problem is not that most students plan to get into trouble. The problem is that most students don't plan *not to*. I have never met a student who planned to:

✓ Drift away from the Lord

✓ Get pregnant

✓ Become addicted to alcohol or tobacco

✓ Become alienated from Mom or Dad

✓ Be arrested

✓ Ruin his or her reputation

But I have met hundreds of students who didn't plan not to. Wisdom is God's plan to protect our kids from the things that have the potential to destroy their lives. Walking wisely is planning *not to*.

Compasses for Life

What our students need to help them stay on the right course through life's journey are internal "compasses." Asking the question "Is this the wise thing to do?" must become so ingrained in their hearts and minds that it becomes a natural reaction when they are presented with choices.

Past Experiences

The past is one tool that can serve as a compass for the present. Wise students will learn to evaluate opportunities, invitations, and relationships based upon their past experiences. Someone once said that example and experience are the greatest schools of humanity. A student's past experiences are not just fodder for guilt or bad memories. The past can also serve as a compass for the present. Students who are committed to walking wisely must learn how to use the compass of experience to guide them into the future.

I remember the time a ninth grader walked up to me and said he needed to talk. I'll refer to him as Sam. Sam confessed he had a "drinking problem." I knew him pretty well and had serious doubts that he was teetering on the edge of alcoholism. So I asked him to explain. Here is the gist of his story.

Every Friday night after the football game, Sam and his buddies would be dropped off at the local pizza place. Their habit was to make sure they snagged the booth right behind the one occupied by Sam's friend's big brother and his clan. His big brother would order a pitcher of beer, pour a couple of glasses, and pass them back to Sam and his friends.

Sam described the battle he fought every Friday as he would sit there and try not to sip a beer. "Sometimes I could make it through the whole night. But most of the time, I joined in with everybody else." He swore up and down that he never got drunk. But he knew he had no business drinking. Then he looked at me and said, "What do you think I should do?"

Unfortunately for Sam, I was all too ready with an answer. "Quit going to get pizza with your friends after the football game." As expected, he looked at me like I was crazy.

"But what's wrong with getting pizza with my friends?" he asked. "Nothing," I said. "But that's not really the issue. The issue is, in light of your past experience, what is the wise thing to do?" He shrugged his shoulders, said he would think about it, and walked off.

Our students must understand that our experiences dictate what is and isn't wise for each of us. Consequently, this principle is going to work its way out in their lives in unique and specific ways. What is wise for one is not always wise for another.

What About Now?

Current events are also a factor in determining what is and isn't wise. So students must ask, "In light of what's happening around me right now, what is the wise thing to do?" After all, we are all more vulnerable at certain times than others. What's wise today may not be wise tomorrow.

Students are particularly vulnerable to temptation:

- ✓ Right after an argument with their parents

- ✓ Right after final exams

- ✓ During spring break

- ✓ Right after a break-up

- ✓ During family conflict

- ✓ Immediately upon entering a new school

These times of transition call for a heightened commitment to doing the wise thing. Students need to understand the relationship between stressful transitions and their vulnerability. Again, they must learn to ask, "In light of what's happening around me right now, what is the wise thing to do?"

I was reminded of this principle several summers ago when I used to drive with students to summer camp. There were two eleventh-grade girls sitting directly behind me. They were lost in conversation and obviously had no idea that I could hear everything they were saying. Eventually, the conversation turned to boys—then to a somewhat explicit conversation of how far each was willing to go with their boyfriends. I knew this wasn't really any of my business. But like a good pastor, I turned down the radio, pushed back in my seat, and listened in. Here's how the conversation ended . . . minus the unnecessary details.

"Would you let Jeremy . . . ?" [long pause] "Well, if I just had a fight with my mom, I might."

I almost drove off the road. Everything in me wanted to turn around and say, "What does having a fight with your mom have to do with it?" But after I thought about it for a while, it made sense. I had seen this twisted reasoning work itself out in other environments.

Students often attempt to "get back" at their parents by doing self-destructive things. It doesn't make any sense, but that's how their adolescent minds work. Consequently, they are more vulnerable at some junctures than others. This is why we must teach them to ask the wisdom question within the context of their immediate surroundings and emotional states.

✓ In light of what I have just been through, what is the wise thing to do?

✓ In light of what is going on at home, what is the wise thing to do?

✓ In light of what I'm feeling, what is the wise thing to do?

✓ In light of what's happening academically, what is the wise thing to do?

Looking Ahead

The future is also a compass for determining how to walk wisely. In many ways, students are determining today how their tomorrows will look and feel. They are writing the stories they will tell their future spouses. They are writing the stories they will tell their children. They are making decisions now that will determine their self-esteem as adults. They are making decisions now that will determine the kinds of people that will want to associate with them in the future. They are making decisions now that will determine where they will work and how much money they will make.

As our students begin to develop a mental image of what could and should be in their futures, they must ask, "In light of my future hopes and dreams, what is the wise thing to do?" We must help them understand that wisdom is God's way of protecting their dreams. The way of wisdom is the surest path toward the fulfillment of all they long for in the future.

There's a Catch

There is a catch to students living a life of wisdom, however. Students who choose to walk wisely are going to look a little strange to their friends. Even some of their Christian friends won't understand why they would choose to "miss out" on what may appear to be good opportunities. They may be accused of being too legalistic and hung up on rules.

When I teach this principle, I always address this issue. At the end of the lesson, I have them repeat the following phrase aloud: "For me, that just isn't the wise thing to do."

Our students need to know that it is not their responsibility to justify their standards in the eyes of their friends. Their responsibility is to do what is wise. When questioned or criticized, all they need to say is, "For me, that just isn't the wise thing to do." How do you argue with that?

The Benefits of Wisdom

As I mentioned in checkpoint #4, one of the most productive series I did was built around the three types of people mentioned in the book of Proverbs: the wise, the fool, and the scoffer. I used a concordance to look up every verse in Proverbs that mentions these characters. Then I made a list of the terms and phrases that describe each. In addition, I made a list of the consequences or blessings associated with each one.

The following is an abbreviated list of the blessings associated with the person who chooses the path of wisdom.

The wise student:

✓ Makes good decisions (1:1–5)

✓ Will live longer (9:11)

✓ Will be attractive to others (11:30)

✓ Will be wealthy (14:24)

✓ Will be persuasive (16:23)

✓ Will be prepared for the future (21:20)

✓ Will be sought after by those of power and influence (14:35)

✓ Will ultimately rise to a position of power (17:2)

✓ Will be delivered from destruction (28:26)

✓ Will be a good counselor (16:4)

With only a handful of these verses, you should be able to make a compelling argument for the benefits of walking wisely.

The Options

There are alternatives to walking wisely. Students need to know about these as well. They need to know that if they decide not to embrace wisdom as a guiding principle in their lives, they, by default, opt for something else. You never walk away from something without walking toward something else.

As I mentioned, the book of Proverbs describes three categories of people: the wise, the fool, and the scoffer. In addition to describing the benefits of walking wisely, our students need to be familiar with the consequences of choosing either of the other two options.

Option #1: The Fool

Fools are people that know right from wrong but choose to do what is wrong. They couldn't care less about doing right. Fools are directed by their immediate desires. They do what they feel like doing. They are not guided by a predetermined standard of behavior. They go with the emotional flow. Fools generally don't have reasons to explain their behavior. They just do what they want to do regardless of the consequences.

Fools will not take instruction because they believe they already know everything. The writer of Proverbs gives us a vivid word picture of how a fool receives wise counsel when he writes, *"it hangs limp like a lame man's leg in his mouth."*

Just as he outlined the benefits of walking wisely, the writer of Proverbs also describes in detail the consequences of choosing the path of the fool. I would encourage you to do an Internet search and do a little study of your own. List the terms and phrases that describe the outcome of the life of folly. This simple study will provide you and your students with dozens of compelling reasons to flee the way of the fool.

Option #2: The Scoffer

Scoffers, like fools, know right from wrong. And, like the fools, scoffers choose to do wrong. But the scoffers take it a step further. They criticize the wise.

If you have been in student ministry for even a short time, you have run into a scoffer or two. They are the students who present themselves as way too cool for everyone else in the group. They refuse to worship. They refuse to participate in Bible study. What's worse, they look for opportunities to make fun of the students who do. They are arrogant, smart-mouthed, and condescending. They are the ones who consistently ridicule other students for trying to do what's right.

The writer of Proverbs goes so far as to say they are "stupid" (Proverbs 12:1). Consequently, scoffers begin to make very unwise decisions. Their decisions often lead them in downward spirals that culminate in tragedy. When scoffers need wisdom most, it is nowhere to be found. In their attempts to distance themselves from wise people, they distance themselves from wisdom. And, ultimately, that comes back to haunt them.

Every student I have visited in an alcohol- or drug-rehabilitation program, every pregnant teenager I have met, every inmate I have spoken to in depth about his situation has in some way admitted to making "stupid" decisions. And they all thought they were too smart and too careful to get burned. Such is the story of the scoffer.

Our students need to know their options. They need to know that to refuse the path of wisdom is to choose the way of the fool or scoffer. They need to understand the benefits of walking wisely. And they need to understand the consequences of choosing differently.

Taking the First Step

Wisdom begins with the recognition of who God is. The writer of Proverbs says it this way, *"The fear of the LORD is the beginning of wisdom, and the knowledge of the Holy One is understanding"* (9:10 NASB). To fear the Lord is to say, "You are God, and I'm not. You are the teacher, and I am the student. Tell me what to do, and I will do it. I surrender all."

Leading our students to embrace the way of wisdom begins by introducing them to God for who he is: an omniscient, loving, heavenly Father who by nature of his position deserves their loyalty and submission. Wisdom begins when they say yes to God before they know what it is that he requires.

Our students live in a dangerous world. God has promised to protect them if they choose the path of wisdom. As leaders, let's do all we can to instill in our students a hunger to walk wisely.

Checking In

Checkpoint: Wise Choices

Bible Study Assignment

✓ Read Ephesians 5:15–17.

✓ Read Proverbs 28:26.

Questions:

✓ According to Ephesians 5:15–17, why do you think Paul encourages us to be very careful how we live? _____

_____

_____

_____

✓ What is his instruction for living a careful life? _____

_____

_____

_____

✓ Is this a suggestion or a command? _____

_____

_____

_____

✓ According to Proverbs 28:26 (NASB), what is the promise for those who walk wisely?

_____

_____

_____

✓ What does the writer mean by "delivered"? _____

_____

_____

_____

✓ What does a fool trust in? _____

_____

_____

_____

✓ Are you walking with the wise in ministry, or are you a companion of fools? Explain. _____

_____

_____

_____

Checkpoint #6

Ultimate Authority

MAXIMUM FREEDOM, ULTIMATE AUTHORITY

I fight authority . . . authority always wins.

—John Cougar Mellencamp

Concept

Ultimate Authority

Principle

Maximum freedom is found under God's authority.

Critical Question

Are your students submitting to the authorities God has placed over them?

Key Passage

Romans 13:1–2

Ultimate Authority
DILEMMA

Freedom and God do not mix in the minds of most students. In fact, these two entities are as oxymoronic as saying *poor* Bill Gates or *ugly* Angelina Jolie. So when Jesus makes a statement like, *"You will know the truth, and the truth will set you free"* (John 8:32), students immediately dismiss the logic or possible power in such a statement simply because of *who* said it. "God can't possibly be talking about freedom," they reason, "because he is all about rules and regulations." So students ignore this biblical truth and search longingly for a life with little or no authority, hoping to one day find this elusive land of freedom.

Why Authority?

Our students' understanding of ultimate authority is an important checkpoint because so much of their lives revolve around how they respond to authority. How they respond to God's authority will have a direct effect on how they respond to their parents. How they respond to parental authority is directly related to how they respond to the laws that govern us and the people who enforce those laws. How they respond to the people and institutions that enforce the laws of our great nation will determine their standing in society.

Even more important, our students' attitudes toward authority will ultimately affect their intimacy with God. They will also affect how much authority they are entrusted with in their lives.

Marriage is ultimately an authority issue. Parenthood is ultimately an authority issue. Discipleship is ultimately an authority issue. Becoming spiritually influential in the lives of others is ultimately an authority issue.

It may be tempting for students to disregard authority and never attach significance to their attitudes and responses to it. So as their leaders, it is up to us to repeatedly revisit this crucial checkpoint. As we emphasize how the authority issue influences their lives in so many arenas, they will begin to understand why it is important for them to submit to the authorities God has placed over them—and to his ultimate authority. True freedom can be found no other way.

I'm Free!

Adam and Eve were the freest people that ever walked the earth. Why? They lived in a "one rule" world. They were given only one "Thou shalt not." God said they could do whatever they wanted to *except* eat from the tree of the knowledge of good and evil. Tend the garden. Name the animals. Multiply. Just don't touch that tree.

I love to talk to students about the world of Adam and Eve. Like most students, I grew up thinking God loved rules. I assumed he got a kick out of saying no. But in his ideal world—a world that was just the way he wanted it—he only instituted one rule. Why? Because God is not into rules. God loves and values freedom.

Adam and Eve were happy with God's one-rule world until Satan came along and convinced them they could be absolutely free. The implication of his devious line of questioning in the book of Genesis was that God was holding out on them; that there was a level of freedom they were missing. Ultimately, in an attempt to reach for absolute freedom, they chose the way of disobedience and rebellion. The premise of their decision was rebellion brings freedom.

Rebellion was and is the attitude and act of disobeying God's rule. Adam and Eve were convinced that freedom could be found in doing what was forbidden. What they soon realized was that they *lost* their freedom because of their rebellion. No longer would they live in the garden. Adam would have to work for their food. Eve would experience pain in childbearing.

Interestingly enough, our society is full of rules today because of their unwillingness to submit to God's authority. They broke one rule. Now we are inundated with them.

Sound like freedom to you?

There is a significant principle behind God's command to Adam and Eve: *Maximum freedom is found under God's authority.*

That seems so counterintuitive for most students. How can you be under authority *and* free? How can you be following a set of rules, yet have the freedom to choose what you want to do? Isn't that a contradiction? On the surface, it certainly seems to be. But in actuality, it is not.

The Cost of Freedom

Maximum freedom is found under God's authority because God ultimately establishes every authority. Paul, in his letter to the church in Rome, said, *"Everyone must submit himself to the governing authorities, for there is no authority except that which God has established. The authorities that exist have been established by God. Consequently, he who rebels against the authority is rebelling against what God has instituted, and those who do so will bring judgment on themselves"* (Romans 13:1–2).

Peter encouraged his readers to *"submit yourselves for the Lord's sake to every authority instituted among men: whether to the king, as the supreme authority, or to governors, who are sent by him to punish those who do wrong and to commend those who do right"* (1 Peter 2:13–14).

These truths are the backbone of the authority checkpoint. If God is ultimately behind all authority, then authority issues are ultimately spiritual issues. Students cannot pursue intimacy with God and ignore their conflicts with authority. Or to say it another way, students cannot be "right" with God and rebel against the authorities God has placed over them.

Coexist?

Most students believe freedom is a world without authority. That is a lie that robs them of their freedom. Let me illustrate.

Bobby's parents have a set of boundaries that they expect Bobby to adhere to. Nothing unrealistic or dogmatic. Simply a standard to live by. The intention of these boundaries is to keep Bobby out of harm's way and to protect his best interests.

One of those standards is that Bobby will not drink or hang around anyone that has been drinking alcohol, regardless of how good a friend that person may be. Bobby loves his parents and understands what they are trying to do, but he sees their efforts to protect him as overbearing and stifling. None of his friends' parents enforce the same rule, and he is old enough to be responsible.

Bobby decides to disobey his parents' wishes and goes out with his friends one night to party. He doesn't drink that much, but his friends do. On their way home, with a drunken friend at the wheel, their car swerves into the path of a family in a van. The wreck is horrific. Tragically, the mother and three kids in the van are killed instantly. Bobby's friend, who was driving, dies as well.

Let's think about what Bobby's desire for freedom granted him:

1. He lost a friend.

2. He played a part in the death of a woman and her three kids.

3. He saw families devastated for years to come.

4. He broke the law by drinking while under the legal drinking age.

5. He will probably be fined.

6. He may lose his driving privileges.

7. He will lose the trust of his parents.

8. He will lose the trust of his peers.

9. He will probably lose friends.

The list could go on and on. Sound like freedom to you?

Now let's talk about you for a moment. I am going to assume that you are married. (If you aren't, you can dream.) You love your spouse with everything inside of you. He or she is your best friend, lover, and partner in life. There is nothing you wouldn't do for him or her.

When you married your spouse, you vowed to stay married until death. For richer or poorer. In sickness and in health. These are the rules you chose to play by. In essence, when you married your spouse, you said no to every other woman or man on the face of the planet.

What if you decided to cheat on your spouse? Because you wanted freedom, you chose to break the rules of marriage. Let's think about what could result from your choice for freedom versus following the rules:

1. You could lose your marriage.

2. You could lose your friendship with your spouse.

3. You could lose friendship with your spouse's family.

4. You could lose friends.

5. You could lose sex with your spouse.

6. You could lose your children or *at least* time with your children.

7. You could lose money via divorce court, alimony, and child support.

8. You could lose your home or at least some possessions.

And the list could go on and on. Again, sound like freedom to you?

The point is that God wants us to be as free as we can be, but freedom is found *under* authority. Breaking the rules or having no rules at all will not bring freedom. Jesus said that truth sets us free. God is truth, and it is under his authority that we gain freedom.

Rebels Without a Clue

If you had asked me as a teenager what God's favorite word was, my answer would have been simple and quick: No!

In fact, it would have been my humble opinion that the entire Bible could be reduced to that word. (If only narrowing the mammoth truths of Scripture into one concise statement were that easy!) Like many students today, I was convinced that God was a legalistic, outdated geezer with no connection to "real people." His answer, in my mind and in the minds of your students, was and is always no, and the only recourse from such a response is unavoidable rebellion. After all, the universe revolves around me, and it is my right to enjoy this short journey called life.

The teenage years are a transitional time between adolescence and adulthood—from a stage of life with few freedoms and responsibilities to a stage of life with more freedom and responsibilities. During these years, the tendency of most students is to see their authorities as enemies. Parents, police, and pastors are the people who are holding them back from the freedom they feel they deserve—and can handle. In fact, many are even tempted to believe that if they could just get away from home, their battles with authority would end. No more rules! No more "don't do this and don't do that!" In the words of William Wallace from the movie *Braveheart*: "Freeeeeeddddooommm!"

Most teenagers long for the day when they can move out of their houses and be free. As leaders, we wish we could go back! Why? The truth is, the older we get, the more authorities we have over us.

Think about it:

When you were three, who did you have to answer to?

_____

_____

_____

When you entered elementary school, who did you have to answer to?

_____

_____

_____

When you entered middle school and high school, who did you have to answer to?

_____

_____

_____

Now, as an adult, to whom do you have to answer?

_____

_____

_____

There are groups that have only one authority to answer to: men and women in prison. Their only authority is the warden. But that's certainly not freedom!

Our natural stubbornness has a tendency to cry, "I don't want anybody telling me what to do!" But authority is a fact of life. It isn't going away. We can either help students learn to live with it and benefit from it or continue to watch as student after student and graduation class after graduation class resist authority and lose the freedoms they have.

Absolutely—Not!

There is no such thing as absolute freedom. Everybody answers to somebody. Even Jesus.

The Gospels tell us repeatedly about people being in awe of Jesus because of his authority to heal the sick, raise the dead, calm a storm, and command demons to flee. But how did Jesus view his own authority? His interaction with a Roman centurion in Matthew 8 gives us an interesting perspective.

When Jesus had entered Capernaum, a centurion came to him, asking for help. "Lord," he said, "my servant lies at home paralyzed and in terrible suffering."

Jesus said to him, "I will go and heal him."

The centurion replied, "Lord, I do not deserve to have you come under my roof. But just say the word and my servant will be healed. For I myself am a man under authority, with soldiers under me. I tell this one, 'Go,' and he goes; and that one, 'Come,' and he comes. I say to my servant, 'Do this,' and he does it."

When Jesus heard this, he was astonished and said to

those following him, "I tell you the truth, I have not found anyone in Israel with such great faith." *(8:5–10)*

Apparently, this Roman soldier recognized something that many of Christ's closest followers failed to grasp: Jesus himself was under authority. When the centurion gave orders to men below him in rank, those men obeyed because they knew he was operating under the authority of the Roman state. He had authority because he was *under* authority. As he watched Jesus exercise authority over disease and demons, it occurred to him that Christ must be under some divine authority to be able to wield that kind of power.

This short encounter illustrates an important principle: to *have* authority, you must be *under* authority. The authority that Jesus had to heal the sick, raise the dead, and influence weather patterns was granted to him by God. Jesus was under his Father's authority. Consequently, he had authority.

Putting the *Who* Before the *What*

If our students want to have authority, they must learn to live under authority. Every time I teach on this topic, a handful of students will object because their parents or other authorities are not believers and, therefore, are not operating under God's authority. What about the father who is in prison? What about the teacher who seems to love to belittle her students? What about the coach who can't stir up his team without shouting profanities?

Before we can address all the "what abouts," we must first lead our students to embrace the truth of God's ultimate authority. Paul, in his letter to the church in Rome, said: *"Everyone must submit himself to the governing authorities, for there is no authority except that which God has established. The authorities that exist have been established by God. Consequently, he who rebels against the authority is rebelling against what God has instituted, and those who do so will bring judgment on themselves"* (13:1–2).

Similarly, Peter wrote, *"Submit yourselves for the Lord's sake to every authority instituted among men: whether to the king, as the supreme authority, or to governors, who are sent by him to punish those who do wrong and to commend those who do right"* (1 Peter 2:13–14).

It is important for our students to understand that while not every authority is godly, God establishes every authority. Even ungodly authority. Granted, that doesn't make sense on the surface. But the Bible is full of stories that illustrate how God uses ungodly authority to accomplish his purposes. The crucifixion of Christ stands as the paramount example. God's judgment of Israel through the Babylonians is another good example.

Our students will never be able to deal successfully with unjust or ungodly authorities until they submit to God's control over all authority. The issue is not *what* we are being asked to do. The real issue is *who* is asking. When communicating this principle, I state it this way:

Students have a tendency to evaluate rules and requests based on the merit of the rules or requests. If the rule or request makes sense to them or fits in with their plans, they comply. However, if students think that rules or requests are not reasonable or don't make sense or don't fit in with their plans,

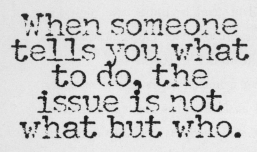

When someone tells you what to do, the issue is not what but who.

they have a tendency to feel it is all right to disobey them.

This explains why a student can waltz in at two a.m. when she knows her curfew is midnight. The rule or request didn't fit with her plans or make sense to her, so she did her own thing. If she's caught, she'll justify her behavior by attacking the rule or the rule maker. "That is a stupid rule! Mom, you are so unfair!"

It is the same reasoning we use to excuse our traffic violations. "Who put that stop sign there?" Or, "This speed limit is unreasonable." In those moments of frustration, it doesn't register with us that God established the governing authorities that determined traffic patterns and speed limits. We focus exclusively on the what rather than the who.

Not a Happy Camper

Rodney was not the kid you would immediately be drawn to as a student minister. In fact, Rodney was the kind of guy most would shy away from. His appearance may have had something to do with it. He seemed to always be wearing his black trench coat, even in the heat of summer, and his "Indiana Jones" hat of choice only deepened his unapproachability and apparent disregard for mankind in general.

What also set Rodney apart from the others is that he never smiled. Even the few times I got close enough to him to have an intelligent conversation, I would walk away with the haunting realization that Rodney was not a happy camper. His beady eyes stared a hole right through me, and the blank look on his face always left me uneasy. He was fixated on hard-core music and the philosophies of Marilyn Manson.

Rodney, in my opinion, was unreachable, and I believed his name would someday appear on a police blotter. Rodney's sister, however, was a very committed believer who loved God passionately. She was very concerned about her brother. One night, because of his sister, Rodney gave this "church deal" a chance, and God spoke to him. I will never forget being pulled into a room and sitting down with Rodney. With tears streaming down his face, he could barely explain what was going on inside. What came out was his story.

I knew that Rodney's mom and dad were divorced, but I didn't know why. It turned out that Rodney's dad was in prison for grand theft. Rodney's father had been his hero—a man he had put his faith and trust in. What poured out of Rodney that night was the anger, frustration, resentment, and distrust that had built up over time. It had shaped Rodney's personality. It had sculpted his moral structure. It had stolen any peace and joy he once had.

Rodney had reduced his image of his father to the criminal he saw him as, and because of this, Rodney had no respect whatsoever for the authorities in his life. He rebelled against his mom. He rebelled against society. He rebelled against his father. He rebelled against God. Anyone the world considered an authority was an enemy to Rodney, including me.

Rodney's story is not unlike those of countless students we interact with every day. Teenagers struggle with the issue of authority—whether they are extremists like Rodney or core students who struggle with obeying their parents. The issue for Rodney was that his father was not a godly authority. The greater issue, however, was Rodney's submission to God's control over *all* authority.

Once Rodney began to understand and embrace this profound truth, we began to see transformation take place. Slowly, but surely, Rodney became more trusting of authority. He gradually allowed God into places that he had kept hidden. He still wears the trench coat and hat, but his submission to God's authority has established a foundation on which other authorities can build in his life.

Get It Right

Let's face it: to rebel against authority is to rebel against God. Our students' attitudes and responses to authority are ultimately their attitudes and responses to God. A student cannot be in rebellion against a God-appointed authority and be in fellowship with God.

If teenagers are rebelling against their parents, for example, they will have a hard time feeling close to God. I can't tell you how many times I've had students come to me, burdened by their lack of intimacy with God, and as I pressed the issue, I discovered that there was tension and rebellion at home. Students can recommit themselves to God repeatedly, but it will be short-lived and eventually fade away until they deal with their attitudes and responses to their parents.

For students to seek God's will about something while in rebellion against authority is futile. We all know students who express sincere passion about their relationship with Christ, but who refuse to come under the authority of their parents. Oftentimes, these kids have a difficult time discerning God's will as it relates to their choices of friends and their plans for the future.

On the other hand, we have all seen students whose spiritual growth suddenly shifted into overdrive when they surrendered to the authorities God had placed in their lives. Looking back, they would agree that the catalysts for their growth spurts were their decisions to acknowledge God's authority in their lives.

To get things right with God, students will have to get things right with Mom and Dad. Those simple acts of submission to authority can be the defining moments for change in their lives.

The Battle Nobody Wins

Teenagers who continue to rebel against authority will find themselves engaged in a never-ending battle they can't win. All the efforts your students make to find ways around the rules will eventually come back to haunt them. A struggle against authority is never ending. Authority doesn't go away. As the great philosopher John Cougar Mellencamp so eloquently says, "I fight authority . . . authority always wins."

Our students need to understand that rebellion always has consequences. God never blesses rebellion. Jonah and his racist heart chose to rebel against God's authority, and he spent several nights inside of Moby Dick, feasting on seaweed and sardines. David and his perverted mind chose to rebel against God's authority, and his rebellion led to a relationship with Bathsheba that evolved into an ancient-day soap opera of murder, illegitimate children, and war.

The real tragedy is that in resisting God's control, our students resist the control of the one who loves them most; the one who has their best interests in mind.

A Better Strategy

In every student ministry, someone raises another issue at this point: What about unjust authorities who require those under their authority to participate in actions that are clearly immoral or illegal? What's a believer to do?

The Scriptures are filled with examples of men and women who were required by their authorities to do things that were in direct conflict with God's commands. What we find in both the Old and New Testaments are men and women who do two things. First, they address their authorities directly with their intentions not to obey. Second, they willingly accept the consequences. The one notable exception is Daniel.

The story of Daniel provides us with a wonderful model for our students. When faced with a command from the king that went against God's law and Daniel's conscience, Daniel made his intentions clear and signaled that he was willing to accept the consequences. But he also suggested an alternative to the king's edict that was agreeable to those in authority over him. He didn't rebel, and he didn't sin.

We can encourage our students to use this strategy when they are asked to do something they find offensive. Suggesting an alternative may very well provide them a way out. For example, what if a teacher asks them to do a report on an objectionable topic? Instead of simply refusing to do the work, they could go to the teacher and suggest an alternative. They must understand, of course, that if the teacher does not accept their proposal, they need to be willing to accept the consequences.

Another option is to appeal to a higher authority (the principal or department head in our example). Paul modeled this strategy after his arrest in Jerusalem. Based on his Roman citizenship, he appealed his case to Rome and was spared a mob trial and painful flogging.

The point is that our students can find ways to stand up for their convictions without resorting to rebellion. The Bible gives them many good examples. If they learn to use these approaches, instead of rebelling, they will learn what it means to find maximum freedom under God's authority.

The Critical Question

The critical question for our leaders is this: are your students submitting to the authorities God has placed over them? We've already shown that our teenagers' attitudes toward authority will affect every facet of their lives. But the issue of authority goes beyond their relationship with the law, school, and family. There are deeper, more fundamental issues at stake. Their attitudes toward authority will affect their ability to trust, submit, and influence others for the rest of their lives.

Trust

Trust is an important, but often missing, ingredient in life. Untrustworthy people have a difficult time trusting. People who can't trust find it impossible to maintain long-term relationships.

Trust, or faith, is also the central concept of Christianity. The heart of our relationship with God is trust. In one sense, faith is a proper reaction to God's authority. Students will only become fully devoted followers of Christ when they learn to trust God as their ultimate authority.

As leaders, we want our students to develop that kind of trust in their heavenly Father. He can do anything. They can follow him anywhere he leads because he will always be there for them. Students who learn to trust God become trustworthy themselves.

Submission

To most Christians, submission is a concept that has more to do with wives and husbands than students. However, submission is first and foremost an attitude pleasing to God. By definition, submission is simply obedience to authority. That makes submission a crucial element in the spiritual growth of our teenagers.

James tells us that wisdom that comes from God is submissive (see James 3:17).

He challenges us to *submit yourselves, then, to God* (James 4:7). In the original Greek language, this imperative command calls for immediate action to root out the sinful attitude of pride.

Many of your students are interested in having victory in their walks with Christ. They want to conquer lust, jealousy, immorality, and gossip. What they struggle with is obedience. We have a tendency to produce events and experiences that facilitate temporary victories, but our goal must be to create environments where obedience to God is the constant standard being raised. God never intended victory to be our goal, but rather obedience. "Victory," states Jerry Bridges, in his book *The Pursuit of Holiness*, "is a byproduct of obedience."

And what is obedience but submission to God's authority and the authorities he establishes?

Influence

Another element that evolves from authority is one we tend to overlook. A proper perspective of authority ultimately earns students influence in the lives of other students. A poor perspective does the opposite. How many students do you know who've been broken over the lost condition of a friend, yet couldn't find the leverage to influence that friend because of some past sin they participated in together? In the mind of the lost friend, God can't be that great if those who claim to be Christians won't submit to God.

Peter admonishes us to "submit yourselves . . . to every authority" (1 Peter 2:13).

When we do, we "silence the ignorant talk of foolish men" (v. 15).

Students who respond properly to authority can counter the false charges their peers make against Christians and are able to commend the gospel to their unbelieving friends.

Practice Makes Perfect

One of the best ways I've found to help students develop the proper perspective on authority is to have mature students accept leadership roles in our ministries. Having college students work with high school students, high school students with middle school students, and so on, creates a dynamic of experiential learning that is invaluable.

At our campuses, we strategically place high school students in areas of ministry on Sunday mornings. Among other things, our students serve on technical support and worship teams in our children's ministry, as well as lead small discipleship groups of middle school kids. These are controlled environments that offer students the freedom to exercise their leadership gifts. At the same time, they learn to submit to the authorities over them. Through serving and leading, the students are placed in positions of authority *under* authority.

Maintaining Your Authority with Students

Perhaps the greatest roadblock we face in talking to students about authority is the seemingly epidemic of fallen authorities in our culture today. Students tend to reason that authority figures who prove to be ungodly forfeit their positions of authority. From religious leaders to athletes to the highest office in our country, the imperfections of those we've held in high regard have undermined the concept of authority among our teenagers.

This is not a new phenomenon. Authority figures have been falling from grace for hundreds and thousands of years.

Consider Moses, whose resume would include: deliverer of God's people and murderer. Or David: a man after God's own heart and adulterer and murderer. Or maybe Thomas Jefferson: writer of the Declaration of Independence and adulterer and father of illegitimate slave children. All great men—but not exactly model citizens.

A few years ago rock star Marilyn Manson wrote in *Rolling Stone*, "Times have not become more violent. They have just become *more televised*" ("Columbine: Whose Fault Is It?" emphasis added).

The essence of his statement is true in relation to the hypocrisy of authority figures. It is not that people in positions of authority are becoming more immoral and imperfect. It is simply that the mistakes of authority figures are more publicized. Students reason that if an authority figure is ungodly, then he has lost his position of authority.

Unfortunately, we can't protect our students from the fact that people will fail us. You and I have no control over the actions of a pastor in New York City or Los Angeles. What we can do is maintain *our* authority with students.

Being under authority as a youth leader has taught me invaluable lessons about the power of authority and maintaining that authority with students. Much of your success in investing the authority checkpoint in the life of a student will rest in your ability to maintain authority with that student. You'll need the following attitudes to gain your students' trust.

Authenticity

Students are not expecting perfection from us. They have the rare ability, unlike adults, to not expect more from others than they do from themselves. What they do demand is authenticity. An authority figure who is not real will not be effective. I have seen this displayed with police officers trying to gain control of volatile situations with students. It is the authentic, transparent officer who gains the respect of students, never the one that thinks he is God's gift to the SWAT team. Authenticity is crucial.

Consistency

Where we go and what we do advertises who we are. The gods we serve paint themselves on our lives. Students see these things, and they aren't fooled.

Hypocrisy in an authority figure is deadly. It may be the thing teenagers hate the most. Students quickly dismiss "do what I say, not what I do" leadership. They want to see consistency between our words and actions, between what we say we believe and how we live. Then they'll listen.

Giftedness

I mention giftedness, not because it is a critical trait for a student leader, but because many leaders make the fatal mistake of assuming their giftedness determines their effectiveness as an authority figure. If authenticity and consistency are the foundation, giftedness is optional, they assume.

It has been my observation that leaders who lack authenticity or struggle with hypocrisy tend to lean on their giftedness as a means to the end. They want to have authority with their students, and they use creativity and imagination to try to get it. But students never believe the hype; they endure. And if the leader is not pure, teenagers will be out of your student ministry in the blink of an eye.

Relationship

How many times have you watched small-group leaders lose their passion for working with students because they used their positions as leverage with their students rather than relationally connecting with them? Leaders who cling to and manipulate their positions eventually lose their positions.

If we want to be influential, our authority must be based on our relationships. You might say that our relationships with our students serve as cushions of love and trust that break their falls when we must exercise truth and authority in their lives.

Respect

Connected to relational authority is the concept of respect. I'm not talking about students respecting us; I'm talking about us respecting our students. Teenagers have valid opinions. Their pains and experiences far exceed anything we can imagine. They are members of a postmodern, electronic generation that learns through multisensory experience and stimulation. (By the way, many students diagnosed with attention deficit disorder are multisensory learners in need of total learning experiences that involve more than just reading books or listening to lectures.) We also need to respect their opinions and personal expressions of individuality, which will allow us to hold a place of authority in their lives.

Here's the bottom line: Unless we learn to live consistent, authentic lives void of hypocrisy; unless we learn to use our giftedness as a tool while refusing to lean on it; and unless we develop real relationships with our students that respect them for the unique and important creations they are, our authority is doomed. Our influence will be short-lived. We will have little success in molding and shaping the spiritual leaders of tomorrow.

Down with the Ship

The movie *U-571* is a white-knuckle World War II suspense drama about an American submarine crew's battle against time and their own fears while carrying out a daring mission to capture a top-secret encrypting device from a Nazi U-boat. It had me on the edge of my seat!

Following an unexpected turn of events, this group of American sailors becomes trapped in the enemy's vessel, deep in hostile waters, and at a major disadvantage because they don't know how to operate the foreign sub. The destiny of these nine ordinary men, as well as the fate of their mission, will ultimately depend on their camaraderie, their instincts, their battle against time and their own fears, and their ability to submit to authority.

In one of the last and most memorable scenes of the movie, Lt. Andrew Tyler pleads with Trigger, a young enlisted sailor, to try one last time to accomplish a seemingly impossible task. A valve that is leaking has rendered the only available torpedo chamber useless. The valve is under several feet of water, and Trigger is the only member of the crew small enough to get to the valve. With an air hose stuck in his mouth, he tries several times to reach the valve, but the air hose won't reach far enough, and heavy debris keeps the valve inches away from Trigger's outstretched fingers.

Trigger weeps, realizing that the enemy is literally seconds from destroying their submarine and he is the crew's last hope.

Lt. Tyler grabs the young sailor and passionately challenges Trigger with these words: "As your commanding officer, I am ordering you to go back and try, because it is your job!" The outcome of the story hinges on Trigger's response to that challenge . . . and, well . . . go see the movie!

If you are like me, there have been times when you wanted to have that kind of leverage with teenagers. Fringe students wander through life with seemingly no guide or conscience, and your core students continually battle with the same struggles as their lost friends. You want to grab them and scream; "I know what I am talking about! You can do this! Your life depends on it! TRY!"

The life of every student is a movie in the making. The outcomes of their stories hinge on their willingness to respond appropriately to the authorities God has placed over them. Live as men and women under authority. And do all you can to instill in the hearts of your students the desire to do the same.

Ultimately, they will be respecting and appreciating God.

Checking In
Checkpoint: Authority

Bible Study Assignment

1. Read the story of paying taxes to Caesar in Matthew 22:15–22.

2. Read the first chapter of Nehemiah.

Questions:

✓ What was the relationship between Nehemiah's position and King Artaxerxes's court and God's ultimate plan for Nehemiah?

_____

_____

_____

✓ What is the principle that Jesus was getting at when he made his statement about the denarius to the Pharisees? If you were going to teach on this passage, how would you state it? _____

_____

_____

_____

✓ Why is it so difficult to stay under authority as a leader? ___

_____

_____

_____

✓ Why do leaders often fear authority? _____

_____

_____

_____

✓ Why is it important that we learn to stay under authority?___

_____

_____

_____

✓ What is the relationship between what God may ultimately want to do *through* you and the authorities he places *over* you?

_____

_____

_____

✓ What have you learned from current or past authorities?

_____

_____

_____

✓ How well do you respond to authority? _____

_____

_____

_____

✓ List some positive characteristics that can easily be misinterpreted by authorities as rebellion in a follower who is a leader.

_____

_____

_____

Checkpoint #7

Others First

CONSIDERING OTHERS BEFORE YOURSELF

The high destiny of the individual is to serve rather than to rule.

—Albert Einstein

Checkpoint

Others First

Critical Question

Do your students consider others before themselves?

Principle

Considering others before yourself.

Key Passage

Philippians 2:3–11

Others First
DILEMMA

Student leaders face a monumental task: developing students who consider others before themselves. Why is this so difficult? Read the headlines. A professional athlete has his girlfriend killed so she won't be able to deliver his baby. Two men on a sinking fishing boat fight over the only life jacket on board, to the point that one man stabs the other and throws him overboard. A teenage girl attending her high-school prom delivers her baby in the ladies' room and leaves the newborn in the toilet to die. The stories go on and on.

Clearly, we live in a very selfish, self-centered society. Most of us have grown so accustomed to our me-first culture that we are suspicious of anyone who demonstrates a genuine others-first attitude.

Combine sinful human nature with a culture that is constantly asking, "What's in it for me?" and it is no wonder that most of our students suffer from a life-threatening case of me-itis. As far as they are concerned, they are the centers of the universe. Their worlds revolve around them. That perception is compounded, of course, by the fact that they often have too much free time, too few responsibilities, and, in many cases, too much money.

The Root of the Conflict

But self-centeredness comes with a price. It is almost impossible to have a genuine relationship with a self-absorbed individual. Our students are paying relationally for the "privilege" of living in their me-first worlds. James went to the heart of the matter when he wrote: *"What causes fights and quarrels among you? Don't they come from your desires that battle within you? You want something but don't get it. You kill and covet, but you cannot have what you want. You quarrel and fight. You do not have, because you do not ask God"* (4:1–2).

The root of all relational conflict is really quite simple: somebody is not getting his or her own way. When getting my way becomes my preoccupation, I have set myself up for a future of friction. As long as I put me first, it is only a matter of time until I run into someone who wants to put himself or herself first. The result, according to James, is "fights and quarrels."

Like all of us, students are prone to blame their relational difficulties on circumstances or on the people they are in conflict with. But the root of their conflict is not circumstantial. The root is that they are not getting what they want.

How do we introduce this not-so-popular principle to our students? One method is to call a student up front and dissect his or her last blowup with Mom or Dad. After the student finishes describing what happened, ask, "What did you want?" Then conclude with this statement: "So the real reason you got mad is that you didn't get your way."

No doubt the student will try to argue the merits of his or her position. Most students will want to leave the impression that they really wanted to do the "right" thing, while what their parents wanted was "wrong." But if you keep the interchange going long enough, it will become apparent that the real issue is that somebody was not getting his or her way.

We all want to be crusaders for what is right. But the truth is, most of us crusade for what we want. Selfishness is like every other appetite: the more you feed it, the bigger and hungrier it gets. As C. S. Lewis stated, an appetite "grows by indulgence. Starving men may think much about food, but so do gluttons."

Self-centeredness is not something that is ever finally and completely satisfied. The more aggressive it gets, the more it wants.

The Root of the Conflict

As Christians, however, our students have been called to a different standard—one that requires them to put the interests of others ahead of their own. The apostle Paul addresses this principle in his letter to the Philippians:

Do nothing out of selfish ambition or vain conceit, but in humility consider others better than yourselves. Each of you should look not only to your own interests, but also to the interests of others.

> Your attitude should be the same as that of Christ Jesus: Who, being in very nature God, did not consider equality with God something to be grasped, but made himself nothing, taking the very nature of a servant, being made in human likeness. And being found in appearance as a man, he humbled himself and became obedient to death—even death on a cross! *(2:3–8)*

These challenging verses contain four overlapping commands. A careful look at each of these reveals both the root of the me-first orientation and some clues as to how we can help our students break free.

1. Don't allow ambition or conceit to drive your decisions.

Teenagers live in a world that is fueled by what Paul refers to as "vain conceit." Vain conceit is the mistaken notion that we deserve special consideration because of something inherently special about us. Directing our students toward an others-first orientation involves exposing the flawed assumption that they deserve special consideration for simply being who they are.

Are all our students unique and special in the eyes of God? Certainly. Does their uniqueness entitle them to special treatment at the expense of others? No.

2. View others as more important than yourself.

Notice Paul never says that one person is better than another; rather, he says that we are to *treat* others as if they were better or more important than us. In other words, our students are to treat their parents, friends, teachers, and leaders as if those people were actually in a league that demands better-than-average treatment.

When I communicate this concept to students, I ask them to close their eyes and picture someone they have never met but whom they admire—for example, an actor, musician, or sports hero. Once they all have someone in mind, I ask them to imagine how they would treat that person if he or she were to come to their house for dinner. What would they talk about? Would they ask questions or sit silently? If the guest asked them to do something, how would they respond?

You get the point. If our students were visited by someone they considered more important than themselves, they would treat that person as a valued individual. That's how they should treat all the people around them! Some students will argue, "But no one is better than anyone else." Remember, Paul isn't arguing that anyone is actually better or superior. Students simply must consider or treat the people around them as if they were better. After all, isn't that what Jesus did?

3. Look out for the interests of others.

This third command is intensely practical. We must not be consumed with our own interests; instead, we must take a genuine interest in the things that interest others. Our students need to understand that their interests are not unimportant or inferior in nature. But when it comes to how they treat others, they are to make others interests the priority. Instead of always talking about themselves and their own needs, schedules, fears, hurts, dreams, accomplishments, and challenges, they need to learn to focus on the needs, schedules, fears, hurts, dreams, accomplishments, and challenges of the people around them.

4. Follow Christ's example of humility.

When challenged to put others first, all of us are quick to make excuses for our preoccupation with self. Most of our excuses are focused on the "unworthiness" of the people around us.

"If you saw how my mom treated me . . ."

"My dad never has time for me; why should I put him first?"

"None of my friends express much interest in how I feel; why should I care about their feelings?"

"They don't treat me with respect; why should I be polite?"

The apostle Paul must have anticipated these objections. To support his exhortations to put others first, he points us in the direction of the supreme example of selflessness: Jesus Christ.

When it comes to our behavior toward others, we are to take our cues from Christ. Literally, we are to have the same perspective and attributes as Christ.

To help our students understand this point, we need to take them on a journey through the life of Christ, focusing on how he treated the people around him. Such a study removes all excuses. Jesus consistently treated others as if they were more important than him—even though they were not. He never pulled rank. He never said, "Since I am God's Son, you must treat me as such." He played by the rules of humanity by choice, not necessity. He constantly laid aside his rights. He was a King who never demanded the deference and courtesy due royalty.

Not only that, he was constantly serving people: washing feet, healing the sick, comforting the brokenhearted. He never allowed the rejection of others to dilute his love and concern for them. Instead, Jesus harnessed everything that set him apart from others in order to benefit the people around him.

Jesus willingly submitted himself to the will of others. Think about it. The Creator subjected himself to the creation! How far did he take his submission? How far was he willing to bend? The apostle Paul put it bluntly: *"He humbled himself and became obedient to death—even death on a cross!"* At Calvary, Jesus put the interests of each of our students ahead of his own. His desire for a relationship with each one of them was more important to him than getting what he deserved.

A Supernatural Attitude

Like most of us, our students were not born as selfless beings. No teenager can do a selfless act of service and truthfully say, "Oh, it came naturally to me." We all have a bent toward selfishness—and that bent is rooted in sin. Because of this bent, serving others has to be an attitude that students develop. They have to be motivated to consider others before themselves.

But how? A servant attitude is supernatural. That's why we need to keep pointing our students to Jesus—the only supernatural human being who ever lived. Although Jesus was equal to God, he did not consider equality with God something he needed to hang on to. His position was not something so important to him that he couldn't stand to lay it aside. His power was not something so precious to him that he couldn't go without it.

What was precious to Jesus? People. Jesus considered people more important than all the power or position in the world. And he wants our students to have that same priority. We need to challenge our students with these questions:

✓ Is your schedule of activities more important than serving others?

✓ Is the position you have among your peers more important than serving others?

✓ **Is your ego or pride keeping you from stooping to serve?**

The Bible says that Jesus "made himself nothing." That puts our students on a level field. A servant attitude really is possible! Jesus had to do the same thing that they have to do to serve: make themselves nothing.

Of course, students need to understand that to say they are "nothing" doesn't mean they are not worth anything. To the contrary, it means that their worth is not for themselves; it is for others. The attitude of a servant is a heart and mind that says, "My life exists for others."

The wonderful paradox is that by living their lives as if they are nothing, students become something in God's eyes. Greatness in this world comes from many things—power, prestige, wealth, fame. But teenagers need to know that greatness in the kingdom of God comes only through serving others. It comes only when they humble themselves and consider the needs of others before their own.

Somebody Has to Go First

It may seem obvious, but we need to remind our students that only one person can go first. Don't rush by this point too fast! When standing at the door, only one person can go through first. When ordering lunch, only one person can order first.

When determining who is going to talk and who is going to listen, only one person can speak first. When two people disagree and there appears to be no compromise, only one person is going to get his or her way.

Either I go first or I allow you to. If I go first and make you wait, there is potential for conflict. But if I let you go first, then there is potential for relationship. And in God's economy, relationship—even the potential for relationship—takes precedence over going first. Demanding my own way will never enrich or further my relationships. On the contrary, the more "rights oriented" I become, the greater my inability to maintain long-term relationships. Selfishness is the enemy of relationship; ultimately, it destroys families, friendships, teams, and churches.

The Role of Ministry

Ministry is another tool God often uses to help students get their eyes off themselves. If you have ever taken your students on a mission trip, you have seen this principle in action. Mission trips and service projects have a way of redirecting the attention and affection of even the most self-absorbed teenagers.

Serving God and others doesn't happen by chance. Students don't stumble into ministry. Teenagers never accidentally serve others. Serving only happens when students make a conscious choice to do it.

That is why mission trips and other service-oriented efforts are often such powerful events in their lives. Students discipline their time to spend weeks or months in preparation. They often work to earn money to cover their costs. During that process, they say no to many activities that would normally distract them, and instead they focus their gifts and abilities on their upcoming service. The trip or event itself is very impacting, but a large part of that impact is because of the investment made beforehand.

God has called and equipped all of us to serve one another. And he has blessed each of our teenagers with gifts and abilities that are to be focused on service.

Out of the Box

Too often, leaders are guilty of limiting the scope of student ministry. We're not just talking about student mission trips and service projects. And we're not talking about involving only those teenagers who can speak, sing, or dance. No, if you and I are committed to moving students away from "what's in it for me?" mind-sets, then we must look for ways to involve them in weekly or monthly environments.

That means we can't be too hung up on whether or not they are "mature" enough to minister. We can't be bogged down in multilayered training processes. We just have to get our students involved in serving. We have to push them out of their comfort zones. We must allow them to bump up against the walls of their ignorance and incompetence. We must push them past their limits. For there, in those exhausting and exasperating environments of ministry and service, God is likely to speak to them in ways he is not able to speak anywhere else.

With this in mind, the student ministry at our church launched a program a decade ago called Student Impact. Student Impact is designed to integrate high school students into the mainstream, weekly ministries of the church. As a result, dozens of high school students serve in leadership positions that are traditionally reserved for adults. They lead small groups, operate cameras, park cars, hand out bulletins, play with preschool children, and lead worship.

We've found that creating opportunities for students to minister alongside their parents and other adults goes a long way toward prying them away from their self-centered mind-sets. We've also seen that students who are given the chance to use their gifts to serve the church have an easier time resisting the consumer mentality that so many teenagers bring with them to church. Teenagers involved in Student Impact show up on Sunday mornings ready to give rather than to simply sit back and take it all in. Some leaders hear about Student Impact and think, *Great idea. But I don't have time to start something new!*

Believe me, I am very familiar with the line of thinking that goes: "I don't have time to start a new program. I don't have time to help students develop their gifts and talents. I'm too busy using mine! In fact, my day is consumed with using my teaching and administration gifts. I want to make sure the students under my watch have the opportunity to participate in environments tailored to their needs and wishes. I want to make sure they are happy and want to come back next week. I don't have time to get them involved in ministry. My time is consumed *doing* ministry."

Is it any wonder that Christian teenagers are just as predisposed to self-centeredness as their secular counterparts? A student ministry focused exclusively on dispensing information in environments designed to attract students is contributing to the very problem this checkpoint is addressing! If our student ministries are all about them, then we shouldn't be surprised when they walk away thinking, *It's all about me.* To focus our attention on simply ministering to them is to reinforce the message that they are at the epicenter of all that matters in life. But by appealing to their giftedness and their responsibilities to the body of Christ, we create a healthy alternative to the me-first world they live in.

Calendar Wars

Most students don't serve God and others because, in their minds, they don't have time. We as leaders don't offer consistent opportunities for service in our ministries because of the same issue: we just don't have time. We look at our programs and schedules and just can't seem to find time to provide students with weekly opportunities to serve others. Let's face it: time is a most precious commodity, and many of the things that capture our time are valid and worthy.

If you don't believe me, prove it to yourself by asking one of your students if you can look at his calendar and checkbook. His calendar will tell you what he considers important enough to monopolize his time, and what is monopolizing his time is what is zapping all of his giftedness, talent, passion, and energy. His checkbook . . . I'm sorry, it's the new millennium . . . his Visa account statement will show you what he deems important enough to exhaust his parents' and his own financial resources. I'm sure you will be amazed at his schedule of activities and the amount of money being spent and where it is being spent.

Reserve to Serve

If we are going to develop students that put others first, we must help them reserve space in their lives to serve God. One may argue that all of life should be serving God. That is so true. However, we are ministering to students, simply because of their season of life, that have many necessary things that battle for their time and energies. Jesus doesn't want them to quit school. He wants them to be excellent in academia. God doesn't want your students to *not* have friends. In fact, your students should be serving others and ministering in all these environments and relationships.

Dr. Richard Swenson, in his book *Margin,* uses a mathematical formula to define this idea of margin: Power−Load = Margin.

Putting this into the context of students becoming others-first oriented, the formula translates: all of your students' gifts, abilities, and energies, subtracted by their time constraints, equals the time they have to serve. If you have a student who is extremely gifted and talented, but her schedule and time constraints exceed what she can do, then that student has no margin to serve. On the other hand, if that same student would lessen her load, she would immediately create space to serve God and others. We need to encourage them to ask themselves:

✓ Is there an activity I need to stop?

✓ Is there a relationship I need to slow down?

✓ Are there things in my life that need to be less of a priority?

Change is hard, but students who want to serve God and others must develop and maintain margin in their lives. It is the ultimate antidote to the poison of busyness. Obviously, we are not talking about encouraging teenagers to drop out of school and set up shop at a soup kitchen. But we are talking about helping them prioritize their lives around something other than their own interests and needs. For many of our students, their busyness has diluted their sensitivity to the Spirit of God. They don't have time to listen, so they don't hear. Consequently, our creative lessons and pithy statements just bounce off. Are they interesting? Yes. Do they penetrate? No.

Going Beyond Words

You and I want to raise up a generation of students that is sensitive to the needs of other people, willing to consider the interests of others first, and ready to serve. But let me ask a blunt question: What are you doing about it? Teaching won't get the job done. Simply telling your students not to be self-centered is a waste of time.

No, somewhere in your busy fall, winter, spring, and summer schedules, you must find a way to move your students out of their comfortable, teenager-centered environments and into other people's lives. Don't be content to simply minister to your students. Raise the bar. Redefine success in terms of students *in ministry* rather than students *attending a ministry*. By doing so, you will have positioned yourself as a leader God can use to raise a generation of teenagers that understands what it really means to put others first.

Checking In

Checkpoint: Others First

Bible Study Assignment

1. Read Philippians 2:3–11.

2. Read John 13:2–17.

Questions:

✓ According to Philippians 2:3–11, what does Paul mean when he says that Jesus "did not consider equality with God something to be grasped"?_____

_____

_____

_____

✓ Based on these verses, do you think Jesus was born with the heart of a servant or did he develop it? _____

_____

_____

_____

✓ Why is the fact that Jesus "made himself nothing" so huge? _

_____

_____

_____

✓ What is Paul saying when he says to "consider" others better than yourself?_____

_____

_____

_____

✓ What do you think Paul meant by "selfish ambition" and "vain conceit"? _____

_____

_____

_____

✓ What does verse 4 say about your purpose in life? _____

_____

_____

_____

✓ According to John 13:2–17, what did Jesus mean when he said, "no servant is greater than his master"? (see v. 10) _____

_____

_____

_____

The Seven Checkpoints Strategy

INVESTING FOR THE FUTURE

It is not the will to win that is important,
but the will to *prepare* to win that makes the difference.

—Vince Lombardi

Seven Checkpoints
STRATEGY

Most parents spend eighteen years of hard labor planning for the day when their son or daughter graduates from high school and enters either the world of higher learning or the workplace. The years leading up to that fateful day are spent investing money and time into their children, with the hopes that their investments will pay dividends when graduation day arrives.

When kids enter the student ministry of your church, what will you invest in them? When they graduate from high school, what will they carry to college or the workplace that reflects your three-to-six-year investment? Is it traceable? Is it transferable? Is it relevant? Is it life changing? Perhaps the questions asked at the beginning of this book are timely for you today:

1. If you had an opportunity to permanently imprint anything you wanted on their minds, what would it be?

2. What do your students need to know? What are the irreducible minimums?

3. When everybody else is "doing it," what's going to keep your students from joining in?

4. When your students are sitting in dorm rooms during their first year contemplating their options for the evening, what is the principle or truth that should drift through their minds in those defining moments?

The Seven Checkpoints answers these questions. If you are like me, you cringe when you think about the students who have had a season of life in your ministry yet never experienced the type of intentional investment of the seven principles we are advocating within these pages. We all feel deep regret for our past mistakes in ministry. The greatest mistake we can make, however, is to fail from this point forward to develop students of substance.

Putting the Checkpoints in Context

We have purposefully resisted talking about context up to this point. The truth is that investing these seven principles into the lives of your students will never happen by chance. It must be a purposeful strategy, implemented by you as the leader, that allows these principles to permeate your students. To do that, however, means that we must take a very hard look at how we define discipleship.

The Big Question

The number one question we get from leaders is, "How do you disciple teenagers?" Theologians and scholars have been asking the same perplexing question for years as it relates to people in general. Dietrich Bonhoeffer, in his classic *The Cost of Discipleship*, proposed that "In the modern world it seems so difficult to walk with absolute certainty in the narrow way of ecclesiastical decision and yet remain in the wide open spaces of the universal love of Christ, of the patience, mercy, and 'philanthropy' of God for the weak and the ungodly. Yet somehow or another we must combine the two, or else we shall follow the paths of men. May God grant us joy as we strive earnestly to follow the way of discipleship."

Student ministries have tried to answer this question in a variety of ways, with the tendency being to *program* our students into godliness. The Sunday-school model has been our most concerted effort. After all, most American students who are going to come to church do so on Sundays. Adults who can teach are there at that time as well. Without taking another day out of anyone's schedule, students can grow spiritually in a convenient environment. Still others, in an attempt to facilitate transparency and flexibility, have preferred informal, off-campus meetings between students or groups of students led by adults.

There's nothing inherently wrong with these approaches. But the question is, how successful have we been in deepening our students' personal relationship with Christ through these environments? If you were to ask a student how Sunday school has changed his life, what do you think his response would be? That's a depressing thought!

Mission Minded

As you begin to determine how you want to teach the seven checkpoints, it is important that the mission of your ministry supports intentional and strategic discipleship. We have seen numerous student ministries across the country begin to invest these seven principles into the lives of their students. The greatest struggle many of them face is having a mission that does not uphold the need for the intentional discipleship found in this strategy or, at worst, no mission statement at all.

By mission statement, we mean that you must have a focused, succinct purpose for your ministry and a statement that articulates that purpose. There are many directions in which your ministry could go, and all are worthy. For example: if your ministry is totally focused in the area of missions, then trying to build the seven checkpoints into your ministry will be a difficult task. To disciple students, however, means that your ministry must be focused and aligned in that regard. Have you ever ridden in a car whose tires needed alignment? The car shakes and bucks and may swerve to the left or right on its own. You can have the steering wheel pointed straight, but the car has other ideas. Why? Its tires are not aligned.

Operating by a mission statement will keep your ministry properly aligned.

Checking the Tires

Defining, or should I say redefining, discipleship is critical to developing a strategy that fits your church and student ministry. Our definition of discipleship is simple: people leading other people into a growing relationship with Jesus Christ. To make it something more than that is to destroy the innocence and adventure of spiritual discovery. To make it less than that is to devalue the magnitude of what happens when authentic community takes place. By authentic community, I mean the balance of transparency, intimacy, depth, and interaction that takes place when students engage each other in small groups. We believe sustained life change is best facilitated through authentic community.

We all like to proclaim that discipling students is a core value of our ministries, but a better gauge is our programming—what we spend our time and money on—and the environments we create to facilitate discipleship. Traditional Sunday school and student activities, as most of us know them, do not support authentic community. They *can,* but a major shift in thinking must take place:

✓ A priority must be placed on creating an environment where transparency and authenticity can flourish.

✓ Adult volunteers must make the shift from teachers/
lecturers to mentors.

✓ Adult leaders must be trained in facilitating
conversation as opposed to getting through a lesson
plan.

✓ A shift must be made from the idea of dispersing
information to sharing one central principle.

✓ That same shift must be made from the idea that
students need to hear every verse in the Bible
during their tenures in your ministry to a focus on
understanding key passages.

Please Note:

I am talking about Sunday school, as most of us have known it
and most students have experienced it. There are churches that
have developed this environment to be one of extreme authenticity and intimacy. The fact
remains, however, that those
churches are rare. And, as a
very wise sage once said . . .

"If the horse is dead . . . dismount!"

It is not that program-
ming is bad. In fact, it is the primary method to accomplish the
monumental task of growing students spiritually. Sunday school
is not the enemy, unless it has become a god unto itself. Where

we seem to be failing is in creating the environments that best facilitate life change. In order to create the best environment possible, we have to define what we are trying to accomplish.

Here are several key components for creating environments that will enable you and your leaders to lead students into a growing relationship with Jesus Christ:

✓ *The Seven Checkpoints* strategy is *relationally driven.*

By relationally driven, we mean that the success of students understanding and applying the seven checkpoints relies heavily on the investment of adult volunteers in your students' lives. Programs don't change people . . . *people* change people. There must be an element of teaching that takes place, but the heart of discipleship is authentic community. The context in which the checkpoints are most successfully taught is a small group of students led by a trustworthy adult who models Christ with passion and consistency.

This week, call several of your students who have graduated from high school or college. Ask them what they remember most about your ministry and what made the greatest impact on their lives. I can guarantee you that their answers will involve people, not information. In fact, I would guess that the principles they have built their lives on came about because of a person, maybe even you. I recently overheard the mother of one of my former students (a recent college graduate and now in the working world in Dallas) telling another mom that her daughter keeps a statement I repeated about dating in a visible place in her apartment. She is living by that principle.

✓ *The Seven Checkpoints* strategy is a *process.*

It is fragile thinking to assume that we can deem a student discipled after a year, an eight-week course, or at the completion of certain requirements. Discipleship is never ending. Again, I am afraid we have erred on the programmatic side in this regard. It is a mistake, in my opinion, to overprogram discipleship. Structure is a necessity. A strategy is necessary. But evaluating a student's discipleship by how many quiet times she has in a week, checking her journal, or how many verses she can recite is shaky ground for judging the depth of a student's walk with Christ.

Duffy Robbins, in his book *The Ministry of Nurture*, illustrates this beautifully when he says, "One rarely hears a youth minister aspire to build a youth group of kids who would fall asleep during prayer time. But when given a glimpse of Jesus' disciples during those final hours before his arrest, we see Jesus so earnestly in prayer that he sweats blood. Meanwhile, the three disciples that were probably the closest to him are sound asleep in a flowerbed, perhaps, at best, dreaming about prayer! These are real-life disciples? People will know you are my disciples by the ears you cut off each other?"

✓ *The Seven Checkpoints* strategy is *product minded.*
The result of the seven-checkpoints strategy must be students in a growing relationship with Jesus Christ. Too many of our discipleship programs are more about the program, the literature, or the teaching. The seven-checkpoints strategy must be about the students. As leaders, our target must be what we want those students to look like ten or twenty years in the future. We have a tendency to be consumed with the now. It is obvious why. Parents want their kids to not get pregnant, never get arrested, not to hang out with him or her, not to date that one or this one, make good grades, be responsible, and on and on. As leaders, it's so easy to be sucked into that vacuum and become only present-tense focused. The true test of our influence in a student's life will probably not be traceable until that student has graduated from college and entered adulthood. To become product

minded in your ministry is to be able to minister in the present while always looking to the future.

How Does It Work?

Practically speaking, how does the seven-checkpoints strategy work? *The Seven Checkpoints* strategy is a systematic, intentional approach to discipleship that is driven by content and not context. It is adaptable to any environment available to you and your specific situation. Some environments and values of that environment may need to be tweaked or changed, but the seven-checkpoints strategy can be used in any discipleship environment.

Each checkpoint will be taught two times during middle school and four times during high school. There are subcategories, or bottom lines, under each checkpoint.

- ✓ *Two weeks are subtracted for Christmas and Thanksgiving.*

- ✓ *Five weeks are subtracted for flexible teaching and unknown scheduling conflicts.*

- ✓ *Ten weeks are devoted to two book studies per year. The books of the Bible we choose to study are books that have as a central theme one of the seven checkpoints.*

Character studies can be the basis of some specific focus studies. See our *Suggested Character Studies* below.

Teaching the checkpoints can vary in style and environment. At our campuses, when we say *teach,* we are referring to an environment that looks like this:

1. *Transit,* our middle school discipleship environment, meets on Sunday mornings from 9:00 a.m. to 10:10 a.m. and from 11:00 a.m. to 12:10 p.m.

2. *InsideOut,* our high school discipleship environment, meets on Sunday afternoons from 4:30 to 6:30 p.m.

✓ Worship is important. Our students begin with about thirty minutes of worship and praise. It is the goal of this time to honor and glorify God, while preparing hearts and minds for the checkpoint being taught.

✓ We then teach the checkpoint, using a master teacher, for no more than twenty-five minutes. The master teacher's job is to teach a central principle from a key passage in a memorable, understandable, and applicable way.

✓ Students then break into small groups, divided by gender, grade, and school. Small groups are led by trustworthy adults who model Christ with passion and consistency. They meet for thirty to forty-five minutes.

✓ The small-group leader's job is to facilitate conversation and accountability by using questions geared to stimulate thinking and initiate conversation on the checkpoint just taught. The small-group leader will conclude the small-group time by giving an application challenge for the week based on the checkpoint.

✓ We ask small-group leaders to develop mentor relationships with their students.

✓ In the high school ministry, we "graduate" the small-group leaders with their students each year until their students graduate. The small-group leaders can then receive an incoming class of freshmen.

Do you have to set up your ministry like ours? Absolutely not. When and where you choose to teach the seven checkpoints will depend on your specific situation. For various reasons, it may be that you can't disciple students anywhere but Sunday school. You may choose to do cell groups in homes. You may be able to wipe your proverbial slate clean and start from scratch. What is important is *how* you create the environment for discipleship. Creating the proper environment is critical to the success of any strategy.

At our campuses, we talk about environments in the context of someone visiting your home:

✓ The Foyer Environment

If a total stranger knocked on your door, his first impression of you and your home would be in your foyer. That conversation, as hard as you tried to be warm and friendly, would hover in formality. That is why the foyer of your home needs to be as friendly, warm, and inviting as possible. We compare this to our environment for students who have no clue about God, the Bible, or church. Like you would in your home, we make that environment as friendly, warm, and inviting to a lost person as we can without compromising the truth.

✓ The Living Room Environment

If you invited someone to come in from the cold and sit and talk, you would most likely invite him to join you in your living room. This environment is not as formal as your foyer, but not really the most transparent atmosphere in your home. Conversation may happen, but not at great depths of honesty or disclosure. Unfortunately, whether it is Sunday school or small groups, most student discipleship environments are more like living rooms than places that promote authentic community. That would explain why students don't share, talk, or even listen.

✓ The Kitchen Table Environment
The people you know and trust are usually invited to sit at your kitchen table. Honesty and full disclosure are part of your relationship. I experience some of the greatest moments of truth, honesty, candor, and transparency with my own children at our kitchen table. This is the type of environment that best facilitates the seven checkpoints strategy.

The best environment is really determined by what you want students to remember, understand, and apply. It is shaped by the content of your message. If you want to share introductory ideas about God, the Bible, and Jesus, then create a foyer environment. If you want to go one step deeper, but not experience full disclosure, then create a living room environment. But if you want to have authentic community where real life change can happen, then you must create a kitchen table environment.

If You Build It . . .

Let's talk about the idea of the seven-checkpoints strategy and environments through the grid of student ministry. We believe the goal should be students growing spiritually. With that in mind, your discipleship environment (kitchen table) should be the foundation of your organization. As we have said, this environment can be Sunday school or whatever you determine to be the best environment for authentic community. We feel strongly that small groups are crucial.

Checkpoints in the Foyer

The seven checkpoints can determine not only the content of your discipleship environment but your outreach environments as well. Once you become purposeful with your discipleship environment, the likelihood of a lost student consistently attending that environment will be very low. However, those students will give an outreach (foyer) environment a chance. The seven-checkpoints strategy is set up in such a way as to give you content to communicate during your outreach events as well.

As we stated in the checkpoint overview, at our campuses, we communicate one checkpoint per month in both our outreach and discipleship environments. At *InsideOut* (our discipleship environment), we go much more in-depth, students are challenged, and accountability is high.

Not only can this strategy transform your weekly programs, but your annual events can become purposeful as well.

The Seven Checkpoints can serve as your content, themes, and focus for events like summer camp, retreats, and mission trips. By having a strategy for what you will communicate each year, your planning will become focused and allow you the time to actually minister to students. Your students will have opportunities to focus on critical areas of their lives for extended periods. Creatively, you can become focused on how to communicate effectively the truths represented in each checkpoint, instead of using a cool T-shirt as your inspiration for the direction of your events.

The Measuring Stick

Another question we get frequently from leaders is one about measurement: How do you measure and track success in discipleship? If it is not about how many come, are completing tasks, and sharing their faith with X amount of people each week, how do we measure success? This is a valid question. In fact, your job may depend on it. The answer is simple, although not easy. Most of us have been trained and operate in environments where statistics are the tools for measuring success and failure. "How many" may be the operative words in your world.

Story Time

We think that discipleship is best measured by stories. Since we are talking about the process of a growing relationship with Christ, spiritual growth is best marked by the intricate stories that you hear from lives that are being transformed by truth.

Let's be honest: when your ministry is based on a program, statistics are the obvious source of measurement. However, when the focus of your ministry is people connecting in authentic community, the stories of life change become the marks of progress.

The following is a letter written to one of our small-group leaders by one of the girls in her small group last year. Listen to her story:

I was watching this TV show, *Felicity*, Sunday after church. If you haven't seen it before, it is about this girl in college who runs into all kinds of living problems. In this particular episode, she was learning to cope with change. As she was ending the show, she said something that reminded me of my own situation. She said, "The hardest thing about moving forward is not looking back." I think what really struck me about this is that I do look back. I look back and remember all of the awful things I've done. How could anyone ever forgive me for those things? I can't even forgive myself! On top of that, I don't know how to forgive myself until the people I have hurt the most can forgive me.

Before I was caught for all the terrible things I had been doing, I remember wanting to change. I used to remind myself at least twice a day how much I hated myself. You know what? You are right. God is working on me, and he is using my mom to do it. Now I am sure she does not know that, but I do. She found something in my purse that pretty much gave away exactly what I was doing and where I was headed. You know what she said to me? She said, "Most parents would have probably wished they had never opened up your purse to find those pills, but I am glad I did." At first, I was not sorry for what I had done, but I was sorry that I had been caught. Then I really thought about it. I know God knew I wanted to change because I told him. I obviously needed help though. I believe God asked my mom to find out to help save me. You know what else I believe? That God loves me. He must. He has blessed me with my mom, who is definitely making a huge impact on how and who I am changing into. He has blessed me with North Point, caring friends from work, supportive friends from school, you (for what you have already done for me and will do for me, I will never be able to thank you enough), and many others.

I can't remember when this was, but one week at Rush Hour (our previous outreach environment), we were talking about how God has a purpose for everyone. What do you think my purpose is? Am I supposed to figure that out myself, or will he show me what it is? Maybe my purpose here is to share God's love with others like you do and did when you were my age. I hope so. I have already tried to make it my purpose. It is happening slowly, but it is happening. So, you don't have to worry about me turning my back, because I won't. I guess the conclusion to this journal entry (or whatever I have been writing) is I am ready to give my life to God. I will need some assistance.

Since I have told you, the only person left to tell is him. So I am going to end this entry. I have some big news to tell someone who I'm sure has been waiting a long time to hear.

Is there a better measure for success?

Checking In
The Seven Checkpoints Strategy

Bible Study Assignment

✓ Read all four Gospels.

Questions:

✓ Did Jesus communicate differently in various environments?

_____

_____

_____

✓ Record an example of a foyer environment, a living room environment, and a kitchen table environment from the Gospels.

_____

_____

_____

✓ What are the determining factors that make your ministry situation what it is? _____

_____

_____

_____

✓ Are your adult leaders operating as mentors or teachers? Why? _____

_____

_____

_____

✓ Do your students sense and interact in authentic community in your present discipleship environment? Why or why not? __

_____

_____

_____

✓ Can your mission support the seven-checkpoints strategy? Why or why not? _____

_____

_____

_____

Appendix 1

Seven Checkpoints
for Student Leaders

Three-Year Middle-School Lesson Menu
Year 1

Weeks	Checkpoint	Bottom Lines
1–5	Authentic Faith	What is faith?
6–10	Spiritual Disciplines	Personal time with God
11–15	Moral Boundaries	Dating
16–20	*Book Study*	*Proverbs*
21–25	Meaningful Friendships	Choosing friends
26–30	Wise Choices	Walking wisely
31–35	Ultimate Authority	God's authority
36–40	*Book Study*	*Philippians*
41–45	Others First	Selflessness

Year 2

Weeks	Checkpoint	Bottom Lines
1–5	Authentic Faith	Grace
6–10	Spiritual Disciplines	Authority of Scripture
11–15	Moral Boundaries	Thought life
16–20	*Book Study*	*Daniel*
21–25	Meaningful Friendships	Accountability
26–30	Wise Choices	Will of God
31–35	Ultimate Authority	Servant leadership
36–40	*Book Study*	*Ephesians*
41–45	Others First	Submission

Year 3

Weeks	Checkpoint	Bottom Lines
1–5	Authentic Faith	Trusting God
6–10	Spiritual Disciplines	Prayer
11–15	Moral Boundaries	Character
16–20	*Book Study*	*Jonah*
21–25	Meaningful Friendships	Peer pressure
26–30	Wise Choices	Narrow versus wide road
31–35	Ultimate Authority	Honoring parents
36–40	*Book Study*	*John*
41–45	Others First	Humility

Four-Year High School Lesson Menu

Each checkpoint is taught four times over the course of four years. There are subcategories, or bottom lines, under each checkpoint with which we teach and challenge students each year.

The plan is based on forty-five weeks per year.

✓ Two weeks are subtracted for Christmas and Thanksgiving.

✓ Five weeks are subtracted for flexible teaching and unknown scheduling conflicts.

Ten weeks are devoted to two book studies per year. The books of the Bible we choose to study have as a central theme one of the seven checkpoints.

Character studies can be the basis of some specific focus studies. See our Suggested Character Studies below.

Year 1

Weeks	Checkpoint	Bottom Lines
1–5	Authentic Faith	Salvation
6–10	Spiritual Disciplines	Personal time with God
11–15	Moral Boundaries	Dating
16–20	*Book Study*	*Romans*
21–25	Meaningful Friendships	Influencing unbelievers
26–30	Wise Choices	Decision making

31–35	Ultimate Authority	Parental authority
36–40	*Book Study*	*Philippians*
41–45	Others First	Spiritual gifts

Year 2

Weeks	Checkpoint	Bottom Lines
1–5	Authentic Faith	Grace
6–10	Spiritual Disciplines	Authority of Scripture
11–15	Moral Boundaries	Thought life
16–20	*Book Study*	*James*
21–25	Meaningful Friendships	Accountability
26–30	Wise Choices	Will of God
31–35	Ultimate Authority	Submission
36–40	*Book Study*	*Proverbs*
41–45	Others First	Servant leadership

Year 3

Weeks	Checkpoint	Bottom Lines
1–5	Authentic Faith	Trusting God
6–10	Spiritual Disciplines	Prayer
11–15	Moral Boundaries	Sexual Purity
16–20	*Book Study*	*Philippians*
21–25	Meaningful Friendships	Peer pressure
26–30	Wise Choices	Building character
31–35	Ultimate Authority	Respecting leadership
36–40	*Book Study*	*Psalms*
41–45	Others First	Student impact

Year 4

Weeks	Checkpoint	Bottom Lines
1–5	Authentic Faith	Forgiveness
6–10	Spiritual Disciplines	Intimacy with God
11–15	Moral Boundaries	Sowing and reaping
16–20	*Book Study*	*Hebrews*
21–25	Meaningful Friendships	Becoming a true friend
26–30	Wise Choices	Walking wisely
31–35	Ultimate Authority	Obedience
36–40	*Book Study*	*Ephesians*
41–45	Others First	Others minded

Suggested Character/Book Studies:

Authentic Faith

- Abraham

- Moses

Spiritual Disciplines

- Psalms

- Jesus

Moral Boundaries

- David

- Samson

Appendix 1

Meaningful Friendships

- David and Jonathan

- Paul and Timothy

Wise Choices

- Solomon

- Nehemiah

Ultimate Authority

- Joseph

- Joshua

Others First

- Jesus

Appendix 2

The following lesson plans are samples of the material we've developed at North Point Community Church.

Sample #1

- ✓ Checkpoint #2: Spiritual Disciplines
- ✓ Bottom Line: Quiet Time
- ✓ Session One: Hide and Seek
- ✓ Key Passage: Mark 1:35–37

Principle

Solitude paves the way to quiet time alone with God.

Introduction

How do you create a new perspective on one of the most reviewed principles of spiritual growth in Christianity? What students need to see is that most Christians struggle with the balance between having intimacy with God and the discipline necessary to deliver that intimacy.

God's pursuit of us is based on his desire to be in intimate relationship with us. As in any relationship, you must spend time with him for the relationship to be intimate. And just as with other relationships, the environment in which you spend that time together will determine much of the quality and excellence of that time.

Outline

I. Intimacy can be defined as being fully known by someone and fully knowing that someone without fear of rejection.

A. Intimacy is the goal of spending time with God.

B. God desires a personal, intimate, face-to-face relationship with you.

C. It is possible to be good church people doing good church things for good church reasons and miss this thing that God greatly desires of us.

D. The vibrancy of a Spirit-filled life rests in your choice to spend time with a living, all-powerful God that created you for himself.

II. Today we are exploring one essential element of this elusive time with God: *solitude.*

    A. Henri Nouwen in *The Way of the Heart* says, "Solitude is the furnace of transformation."

    B. Think about these names:

        1. Abraham

        2. Moses

        3. Joshua

        4. Jonah

        5. David

        6. John the Baptist

        7. Paul

        8. Jesus

    C. All of these men have a common thread in their histories: God allowed them to go through an extended time of solitude before they began to influence the world.

    D. We often look at their solitude as a time of punishment.

        1. God looked at their solitude as the environment for transformation in their lives.

        2. God still looks at solitude in the same way.

III. We mentioned in the introduction that time with God seems to be *elusive.*

    A. Time with God is elusive because it hinges on a fleeting component of life: *time.*

    B. Solitude is crucial because in it *you capture time.*

      C. Solitude pushes out distraction and interruption. Life seems to go in slow motion.

      D. The greatest hindrance to meeting with God is distraction.

         1. Solitude creates as much of a "distractionless" environment as possible.

         2. Distractions serve as the enemy of intimacy, our ultimate goal with God.

      E. Jesus considered solitude important in his time with God.

      F. Jesus exemplifies components of solitude that we must understand and embrace.

IV. Solitude captures time.

      A. Verse 35 starts with ten words that most of us detest: *"Very early in the morning while it was still dark . . ."*

      B. Early morning can be the best time to spend time with God.

         1. It is a practical way of applying *"seek first his kingdom and his righteousness"* (Matthew 6:33).

         2. Jesus modeled it.

      C. The principle is what is important: time is the crucial element in solitude.

      D. Whenever you can capture time through solitude, then that is a chance for you to spend intimate time with God.

V. Solitude hinges on environment.

A. Jesus did something that is crucial to solitude: he "left the house and went off to a solitary place."

B. Jesus had a place to go to gain solitude.

   1. The Savior of the world needed a quiet place to go.

   2. With his schedule, he probably scouted out the best "hiding place."

C. All of us have played hide and seek.

   1. Think about those hiding places where no one could find you.

   2. Remember hearing your own heartbeat while you waited for someone to find you?

   3. Remember that you could hear yourself breathing?

   4. Remember that you didn't dare move for fear of being found?

D. Your environment of solitude created all of that.

E. You didn't want to be found . . . neither did Jesus.

VI. Solitude must be purposeful.

A. Why did Jesus get up early in the morning while it was still dark, leave his house, and go off to a solitary place?

   1. Verse 35 concludes with these three words: *"where he prayed."*

   2. Solitude will always seem like a waste of time if there is no purpose in it.

B. Solitude *with* purpose breeds discipline and intimacy.

C. Solitude *without* purpose will breed inconsistency and apathy.

D. Jesus captured time for one reason: *to pursue intimacy with his Father.*

Illustration

I was really convicted when thinking about this idea of capturing time through solitude in order to spend time with God. Think about the trouble you used to go through—and students go through—to be alone with a "significant other." Do you remember how careful you were to arrange your time so that you could meet that person on time? Do you remember all the effort you went through to make sure the two of you were in a solitary place? Why did you go through all that trouble?

To experience intimacy.

May we never slide into a place of complacency when it come to seeking that kind of solitude for intimacy with God.

Small-Group Questions

1. Would you say that you experience intimacy with God? Why or why not?

2. Do you practice a consistent time alone with God? Why or why not?

3. *When* do you spend time with God? Why?

4. *Where* do you spend time with God? Why?

5. *What do you do* in your time alone with God? Why?

6. Read Mark 1:35-37. Do you struggle with getting distracted in your time alone with God? Why or why not?

7. How did God use solitude in the lives of each of the men listed below? What was their solitude?
   - ✓ Abraham
   - ✓ Moses
   - ✓ Joshua
   - ✓ Jonah
   - ✓ David
   - ✓ John the Baptist
   - ✓ Jesus

Sample #2

- ✓ Checkpoint #6: Ultimate Authority
- ✓ Bottom Line: Who's in Charge?
- ✓ Session One: A Fact of Life
- ✓ Key Passage: Romans 13:1-2

Principle

When someone tells you what to do, the issue is not *what* but *who*.

Optional Starter

1. Have students make a list of all the authorities in their lives.

2. Ask them to choose the authority that is the most difficult for them to submit to and put a #1 beside it. Next, have them choose the authority that is the second most difficult to submit to and put a #2 beside it. Have them continue this process until every authority on their list has a number beside it.

3. Ask, "Why is it so hard to submit to the authority you listed as the most difficult to obey?"

   ✓ Is it because you are asked to do things that are wrong?

   ✓ Is it because you are asked to do things that are beyond your abilities?

   ✓ Are the requests unreasonable?

   ✓ Is the problem that you just don't like being told what to do?

4. Most of us believe a big lie when it comes to our clashes with authority. We mistakenly think that the issue is right and wrong. When our authorities ask us to do something we don't want to do, we argue as if what they are asking us to do is wrong. Somewhere along the way we get the notion that we are the ones who want what is right! The truth is, what we really want is our way.

5. It is a mature student who can distinguish between arguing for what is *right* versus arguing for his or her *way*.

Introduction

One of the difficulties about being a student is that you are moving from a stage in life where you had few freedoms and little responsibility to a stage where you have more freedom and greater responsibility. You are becoming an adult. During these years, the tendency is to see your authorities as the enemy—the people that are holding you back from the freedom you think you deserve and are certain you can handle. Maybe you are tempted to believe that if you could just get away from home, your battle with authority would end.

Outline

I. It isn't going to get better.
   A. If you are like most teenagers, you long for the day when you can move out of your house and be free.
   B. The truth is, the older you get, the more authorities you have over you.
      1. When you were three, who did you have to answer to?
      2. When you entered elementary school, who did you have to answer to?
      3. When you entered middle school, the number increased again.
      4. When you leave home, the list of authorities in your life will continue to grow.

    C. There is a group that has only one authority to answer to: men and women in prison.

    D. Authority is a fact of life. It is not going away.

        1. You can learn to live with it and benefit from it, or you can resist it and lose the freedom that you have.

        2. There is no such thing as ultimate freedom.

        3. Everybody answers to somebody.

II. There is one basic thing you need to know about authority: God *ultimately establishes every authority.*

    A. Not every authority is godly, but God establishes every authority.

        1. We are going to talk about ungodly authorities later.

        2. We are going to talk about what to do when asked to do something wrong.

        3. You will never be able to deal successfully with unjust authorities until you submit to God's control over all authority.

    B. To rebel against an authority is to rebel against God.

        1. Your attitude and response to your authorities is ultimately your attitude and response to God.

        2. You cannot be in rebellion against a God-appointed authority and be in fellowship with God.

    C. Rebellion always has consequences.

1. Even rebellion against unfair or unjust authority figures has consequences.

2. God never approves of or blesses rebellion.

III. The real issue is, *who* is asking us to do something, not *what* are we being asked to do.

   A. We tend to evaluate rules and requests based on the merit of the rule or request.

      1. If we think the rule or request is reasonable; if it makes sense to us; if it fits in with our plans; and if it doesn't get in our way . . . then we obey!

      2. But if we don't think the rule or request is reasonable; if it doesn't make sense to us; if it doesn't fit in with our plans; or if it does get in our way . . . then we feel it is okay to disobey!

   B. When we are caught, we justify our behavior by attacking the authority or the rule maker.

   C. If God puts all the authorities in your life, then the issue is not *what* you are being asked to do but *who* is doing the asking.

IV. The first principle of authority is: when someone tells you what to do, the issue is not *what* but *who*.

   A. What this really boils down to is, who is going to be in control of your life?

      1. As long as your obedience is based on rules and requests, you are retaining control.

      2. As long as you are in control, God is not!

B. Ultimately, you cannot win the battle against authority.

    1. Ultimately, you are battling against God—and no one has ever won that struggle!

    2. The real tragedy is that resisting God's control is to resist control of the One who loves you more than anyone else—the One who has your best interests in mind.

Small-Group Questions

1. Read Romans 13:1–2. What does Paul say our response to authority must be?

2. What does Paul say is the consequence of failing to respond to God's authority properly?

3. Do you struggle with authority figures in your life? Why or why not?

4. Do you tend to evaluate rules and requests based on how good the rule or request is from your perspective? Why?

5. What do you think is the danger in evaluating rules?

6. Do you justify wrong behavior by blaming the authority figure or rule maker?

7. Discuss this statement: if God puts all the authorities in your life, then the issue is not *what* you are being asked to do but *who* is doing the asking.

Acknowledgments

Every book represents a team effort. This one is certainly no exception. Without each of the following people, this book would never have happened.

Reggie Joiner, Kevin Ragsdale, Heath Bennett, and Clay Scroggins

Your passion and vision to develop teenagers who make a difference is contagious. Thank you for championing the cause and setting the standard so high! You guys are the real heroes of this project.

Our Families

Thank you for enduring the technology problems, editing issues, late nights, and phone calls. We love you more than you will ever know.

Diane Grant

Thank you for being the world's greatest facilitator of information with such a heart for people. How do you do it?

Denny and Philis Boultinghouse

Thank you for believing in this project.

Michele Buckingham

Thank you for reading between the lines and crossing the *ts*. You are awesome!

About the Authors

About the Authors

Andy Stanley is a pastor, communicator, author, and the founder of North Point Ministries, Inc. (NPM). Since its inception in 1995, NPM has grown from one campus to five in the Atlanta area and has helped plant over twenty-two strategic partner churches throughout the United States. Each Sunday, more than twenty-five thousand adults attend worship services at one of NPM's five campuses: North Point Community Church, Browns Bridge Community Church, Buckhead Church, Watermarke Church, and Gwinnett Church. Andy's books include *The Grace of God, Communicating for a Change, Making Vision Stick, Next Generation Leader, The Principle of the Path,* and *How Good Is Good Enough?* Andy lives in Alpharetta, Georgia, with his wife, Sandra, and their three children.

Stuart Hall provides vision and leadership for two highly effective, nonprofit organizations (XP3 and DASH INC). He deeply desires to develop spiritually influential students who engage culture. Stuart partners with great organizations like the Fellowship of Christian

Athletes to develop students as leaders. He also travels and speaks to thousands of students and leaders each year. Stuart has coauthored three books (*The Seven Checkpoints: Seven Principles Every Teenager Needs to Know*, *MAX Q: Developing Students of Influence* and *Wired: for a Life of Worship, Leaders Edition*). He is working on authoring one or two more books, laughs incessantly, coaches his daughters' basketball teams, relishes watching his kids play sports, and loves his beautiful wife, Kellee, with every fiber of his being.